First-Job

SURVIVAL

GUIDE

Also by Andrea J. Sutcliffe

The New York Public Library
Writer's Guide to Style and Usage (ed.)

Numbers: How Many, How Long, How Far, How Much

First-Job

SURVIVAL

GUIDE

Andrea J. Sutcliffe

AN OWL BOOK

HENRY HOLT

AND COMPANY

NEW YORK

Henry Holt and Company, Inc. *Publishers since 1866*
115 West 18th Street, New York, New York 10011

Henry Holt® is a registered trademark of Henry Holt and Company, Inc.

Published in Canada by Fitzhenry & Whiteside Ltd.,
195 Allstate Parkway, Markham, Ontario L3R 4T8.

Library of Congress Cataloging-in-Publication Data
Sutcliffe, Andrea J.
    First-job survival guide / Andrea J. Sutcliffe. —1st ed.
        p.   cm.
    "An Owl book."
    Includes bibliographical references and index.
        1. Youth—Employment—United States—Case studies.
        2. Vocational guidance— United States—Case studies.   I. Title.
    HD6273.S88   1997   96-37716
    650.14—dc21   CIP

ISBN 0-8050-5014-0

Henry Holt books are available for special promotions and
premiums. For details contact: Director, Special Markets.

First Edition—1997

Designed by Victoria Hartman

Printed in the United States of America
All first editions are printed on acid-free paper. ∞
10 9 8 7 6 5 4 3 2 1

To Stephanie

Acknowledgments

The suggestions and advice in this book were drawn from nearly twenty years of working with young people in their first jobs. Many of the real-life examples and much of the down-to-earth advice for today's twenty-somethings come from three savvy and successful young women: Stephanie De La Garza, Christina Huszcza, and Pamela Sarver. Their recent first-job experiences reflect the realities of today's business world while also proving that some things never change. My sincere thanks go to them.

Many thanks also to Cynthia Vartan, editor-at-large at Henry Holt, and to Ed Sutcliffe, for their support and words of encouragement.

Contents

2 · Why Attitude Matters Most   24

Introduction

You've landed your first real job—congratulations! You're no doubt eager to put your college education or technical training to work and start a satisfying and successful career.

There's just one problem. No one—not your teachers, your parents, your older friends, or your siblings—has told you about the *real* skills and knowledge you'll need to get ahead. It's not that they don't want to; it's just that they hope the things that happened to them won't happen to you, or that they think different things may happen to you. Or it may be that they feel these things are too hard to explain, and that you'll simply have to learn the hard way, just as they did.

But you shouldn't have to learn the hard way, any more than you would have been expected to learn algebra without a teacher or a book. The situations we'll describe are as basic as human nature, and just as hard to fathom at times. But knowledge is power, as they say, and even if all you do is become aware of the kinds of problems and frustrations you'll face in your first year on the job, you'll be ahead of the game.

Here are a few examples of typical first-job problems:

- Your boss brushes off some of your best ideas and gives you grunt work instead.

- Your reports and memos come back to you marked up with endless corrections and suggestions for improvement—and you made A's in English comp.
- Your boss's boss doesn't even seem to know who you are.
- Your boss has recently started to hover over your every movement—doesn't she trust you?
- You've been there a year and there's no talk of a promotion or even new duties.
- Your coworkers paint a pretty negative picture of the company, and you're beginning to wonder if it's time to start looking elsewhere.

If any of these happen to you, you won't be alone—most of us have experienced some or all of these things on the job. Comforting as that is, though, it's not enough. You need to know how to deal with these problems to your advantage, and the best way to do that is to understand why they happen. That means learning a few business facts of life, as well as understanding a little about human nature. Let's begin with your first three months on the job.

First-Job

SURVIVAL

GUIDE

Your First Three Months

Your first three months on the job are important—and they're not. Confusing? Here's what that means.

It *is* important to make a good first impression. Make a bad first impression, and you'll find it very hard to overcome.

It *is not* important to wow everyone with your skills and knowledge at this point. Instead, you should be a sponge for a while and do the best job you can on anything you're given. That part will be easy, because at first you won't have much to do that's very hard. More on that later.

But, you may be asking, aren't first impressions based on superficial things, like appearance and good manners? Aren't they paying me for my brains and my education and my ability to get the job done? Yes, but it's not as simple as that. The reality is that your ability to get along with and gain the respect of your peers and managers is usually more important than anything else—and not just now, but for the rest of your career. Failure to recognize this business fact of life trips up many ambitious, smart young people.

Getting along with others is important because very little of an organization's tasks are accomplished by people working independently. A company's organization chart may show ten or fifteen distinct groups and functions, but it doesn't show how these groups work together and depend on each other. And when people must work together, certain basic human qualities—like trust, respect, courtesy, and helpfulness, or the lack thereof—can make or break even the most promising projects, programs, and careers. Chapter 4, Getting Along with Your Boss and Your Coworkers, explains more about how to deal with and understand the people you work with.

MAKING A GOOD FIRST IMPRESSION

The Way You Look

Like it or not, you will first be judged on how you look. Even though today's business dress is more relaxed than ever, there are certain lines that shouldn't be crossed. Dress codes, formal or otherwise, vary widely among professions and companies, but you can't go wrong by following the classic advice: Dress like the people who are in the next position you are aspiring to. This doesn't mean you have to take out a loan to buy designer clothes; it simply means that you shouldn't wear T-shirts and sneakers when the successful people around you are wearing business suits and polished shoes.

> Tracy, a marketing assistant in a high-tech company, says, "I found that you won't look your best even in expensive clothes if they don't fit right. I'm five feet tall, and clothes off the rack usually need alterations to look right. It's not cheap to have this done, but it's well worth the cost. Not only do you look better, but you send a message that you care about looking like a professional—and this usually results in being treated like one! By the way, if you find yourself wondering whether your outfit is too casual, it probably is."

If you think that someone will tell you if you're dressing inappropriately, you'll probably be wrong. Most managers are extremely uncomfortable commenting on something as personal as appearance and will avoid saying anything unless it's really necessary. For example, if your boss mentions to you that everyone will be wearing a suit for the next day's client presentation, take the hint—he's probably afraid you'll show up in jeans.

But here's the bigger problem. If you insist on displaying your individuality through inappropriate clothes, hair, makeup, or jewelry, you're probably thinking, "It's my right to be who I am." Unfortunately, your manager is thinking, "When's she going to grow up?" The logical next questions are, "She seems so bright, but is she mature enough to handle this important assignment? And how well developed are her judgment skills?"

> "I changed my hairstyle a few months after I started my first real job," says Melissa, a computer programmer. "I went from the curly, permed high school look I'd worn for years to a shorter, neater-looking adult style. I think it sent the message that I was ready to be treated like an adult."

The Way You Talk

You don't want to remind your boss of her seventeen-year-old, who's giving her trouble these days, so it's in your best interest not to talk like a teenager. The last thing you need as you start your career is to be treated like someone's child.

When you speak, do you typically end sentences with a question mark? "So I filled out this form? But I didn't know what you wanted me to put here? So I left it blank? Okay?"

Or do you punctuate sentences with "like" or "you know"? "Like, I finished early, so, you know, like, I started on that other job you gave me." Breaking yourself of these habits won't be easy but will be well worth the effort.

Some young people overapologize for mistakes or interruptions. Saying "I'm sorry" too often at the beginning or the end of a sentence will make you seem unsure of yourself. People are uncomfortable with those who appear meek or unconfident, and frequent apologies seem to reinforce those impressions. Save "I'm sorry" for major flubs.

A little harder to repair are any problems with pronunciation or grammar. Some mispronunciations are mental misspellings of common words, such as *medium* for *median* or *supposably* for *supposedly*. Other problems may be specific to your line of work. Sara, a hardworking sales rep for a high-tech corporation, couldn't figure out why she wasn't getting orders for a new product her company had introduced. It turned out that she had been incorrectly pronouncing certain relevant words and terms when making presentations to her technical customers. Her errors made them question her overall knowledge and competence. They simply didn't believe she knew what she was talking about.

Like Sara, you're probably not aware of these problems, yet they may invisibly hold you back. Is there someone in your company—in Sara's case, the manager in charge of developing the new product—you could practice your pitch with before you embarrass yourself in front of customers?

Jeff, an editorial assistant with a small publisher, says, "Because of my English degree, I'm often tempted to correct people's speech errors, and if I feel close enough to them, I will. Most of the time I don't, though. If you feel you can take the criticism, ask a close friend or colleague to tell you when they notice a grammar or pronunciation mistake you make. You'll benefit in the long run."

Other speech problems can hurt your credibility as well. Do you mumble or speak too quickly or too slowly? Do you have a thick southern accent that amuses your coworkers in Manhattan? Or is your New England accent an oddity in southern California? Regional accents aren't as big a problem as the others we've discussed, but if your career goal is a position high on the corporate ladder, consider that some executives have hired speech specialists to help them shed heavy accents and undesirable speech habits.

If you speak with an accent, or you are talking with someone who has one (at least to your ears)—say, you're from Atlanta and you're on the phone with someone from Boston—try this: Shortly into your conversation, ask the person if he or she can understand you. By asking, you're giving your listener permission to slow you down or ask you to repeat something without feeling embarrassed. (If you have to repeat yourself, take this as a sure sign the listener's having trouble.) For example, many southerners think that northerners speak too quickly, and many northerners have a hard time dealing with a southern drawl.

The Way You Act

Your attitude is the next thing people will notice about you. During your first three months on the job, it will be the most important aspect of your performance. We'll discuss attitude further in Chapter 2, but for now here are the basic characteristics of a positive attitude:

- You're friendly and open.
- You have a positive outlook.
- You show an interest in learning.
- You are enthusiastic about being there.
- You are willing to listen.
- You are quietly confident about your abilities.
- You show up on time, and you show up every day, unless you are truly ill.
- You are courteous to everyone, regardless of their position in the company.
- You spend most of your day working, not talking to coworkers, wandering the halls, playing games on your computer, chatting with friends on the phone, surfing the Internet, or taking long lunches.

Your boss and your coworkers will no doubt give you a warm and friendly welcome your first couple of days on the job. They'll take extra care to show you around, introduce you to people, and fill you in on the ins and outs of office life. Return their courtesies by showing an interest in what they do and by asking lots of questions.

Don't take it personally when this special treatment ends. Everyone has a job to get done, so don't feel abandoned when you find yourself alone at your desk with little to do. You may have to wait awhile until your boss or the person who is training you can get back to you.

Be very careful how you talk to and treat people in support positions—secretaries, administrative assistants, mailroom clerks, computer technicians, and so on. These people can make your job much easier, and they will be glad to do so if they feel you respect and value what they do. Like anyone else, they are sensitive to being talked down to or ordered around, and you should make your requests for help in the nicest and least condescending way possible. Be aware that your youth and your education may be held against you, and perhaps even resented.

If, for example, you know that you will need two hundred copies made of a seventy-five-page report on Friday, let the copy room supervisor or office manager know about it as soon as you do. Strolling in with demands to complete time-consuming tasks at the last minute will quickly earn you the label of inconsiderate boor. Some day there'll be a crisis job that must be done on short notice, and if you've kept unreasonable demands to a minimum, you'll probably find the staff willing to help you out. You might even offer to pitch in and help if you have time; this will earn you many points.

Learn to estimate how long tasks like photocopying, faxing, word processing, envelope stuffing, and so on take to do. Ask the people who regularly do this work for rules of thumb, such as how many copies per hour or how many pages per day they can realistically produce. Having this information will let you plan your schedule and ensure that the support staff will have the time to help you. Since most employees don't bother to do this, you will stand out as someone who cares, and the support staff will be on your side when you need them most.

Doug, a management intern, says, "Not every office has someone who will make copies or send faxes for you. If I need to make a copy, I do it myself. We have a department secretary, but she has more important things to do. She'd probably be insulted if I asked! When in doubt, do it yourself—especially if they show you how to work the equipment. I think your boss will let you know when you should give work to others to do. Just be sure to never take advantage of other people, no matter what position they're in."

Here's something to watch out for in your first few weeks: Beware of the overly friendly coworker who takes you aside and fills you in on all the office gossip and current gripes with management. It seems every office has one employee like that. You will be viewed as fresh meat and a potential ally to someone who could be the office troublemaker. If you believe everything you hear, it might negatively affect your attitude. If you continue to hang out with this person, your image may suffer as well.

UNDERSTANDING THE CORPORATE CULTURE

Corporate culture is a term used to describe the usually unspoken beliefs and attitudes of a company. Some companies, for example, run things by the book, with rules and procedures for everything, even attire (a well-known computer services company once had a written rule that its male employees were not to wear tasseled loafers or green ties, among other things). Most companies are more laid-back and may not even put rules in writing.

In that case, you'll have to be observant and ask questions—because there is always a code of appearance and behavior, written or not.

The corporate culture comes from the top officers and managers of the company. It reflects their views on management (authoritarian or democratic?), customer service (do customers come first?), the value of their employees (do they reward performance or longevity?), and money (are budgets adhered to down to the penny, or can managers get funds as they need them?). You probably sensed some of this at your hiring interview, but it may take months to get a clear picture of a company's beliefs and operating principles. You may even find that your company's stated beliefs don't match real-life operations. In the long run, your comfort level will depend on how well your personal beliefs and values match the company's.

LEARNING THE RULES, WRITTEN AND UNWRITTEN

You've read and understood the written rules in your company's employee manual (or in the handouts that your manager or the Human Resources person gave you). Now you should start to figure out three things: which written rules are strictly followed, which are not, and what the unwritten rules are. Not knowing this information could get you nailed later on, and you'll never think you were doing something wrong.

The best way to find out how serious management is about written rules is to ask your coworkers. Is having an occasional beer or glass of wine at lunch really grounds for dismissal, or is the company's rule against drinking simply meant to discourage frequent liquid lunches? Will you need a doctor's note if you're out with the flu for more than three days, or will your hacking cough be enough to convince your boss that you are really sick? Needless to say, it's best to find the answers to questions like these beforehand, not by direct experience.

Some unwritten rules are a matter of personal and business

ethics. These include personal business conducted on company time, personal use of company supplies and equipment, office romances, and other matters involving personal judgment and ethics. We'll talk more about ethics in Chapter 5.

Taking Time Off

Attitudes toward aspects of your personal life, such as taking time off for doctors' appointments, family events, or personal errands, can vary widely from company to company. Some employers are quite liberal and don't mind so long as you make up the time, while others require that you charge every quarter hour against leave time. Sometimes these decisions are left up to your manager. You'll eventually find out where your company stands, but during your first three months try to keep requests for time off to a minimum. If you have to get your car inspected or see your dentist, make every attempt to do so outside normal business hours. This advice applies even if you see others taking off during the day to run personal errands. The difference is that you are new and are trying to establish the impression that you are devoted to your job.

Vacation time is usually earned from the day you start work, but many companies will not let you take it until you've been on the job for six months or a year. If you have plans that you know will require time off during your first year, let your boss know as soon as possible. The best time to mention it is when you are offered the job. Most managers understand and will try to accommodate you, but they'd rather not be surprised later, when they might have to explain the need for an exception to someone in Human Resources. Again, a lot will depend on the corporate culture where you work.

If you must take days off during your first three months, try to make sure they're not Mondays. Many managers have come to equate frequent Monday absences with weekend hangover problems, and you don't want to be wrongly labeled if your first few days off happen to be Mondays.

Tardiness is also a no-no, but companies vary in their latitude. To some, it's being three minutes late, while to others it's thirty. Play it safe your first three months and arrive early.

> Stephanie recalls a problem with a new employee in her office: "She used to come in at least fifteen minutes late every day. To her way of thinking, this was okay as long as she stayed fifteen minutes later, but she never ran this by her boss. He was a real stickler about being on time. Once he realized what was happening, he talked to her about it. The moral is, get there when they tell you to, not three minutes later. Being on time or even arriving a little early counts for a lot in performance reviews, too."

Office Etiquette

The rules for office etiquette are rarely put in writing, yet they are much more important than they sound. *Etiquette* is defined in the dictionary as "practices and forms prescribed by social convention or by authority." It's a good idea to find out what is considered good etiquette in your company; ignorance will not be viewed as an excuse. Overall, you can't go wrong if you consistently treat others the way you'd like to be treated.

You'll want to learn right away who you can call by first name and who prefers to be addressed by *Mr., Ms.,* or *Mrs.* You'll find that the use of courtesy titles is not necessarily a function of age or position in the company, although those are good starting places when you're not sure. Listen carefully for hints when you're introduced to someone; you'll do even better to note how your coworkers and your boss address people. Of course, the most direct way is to simply ask the person how he or she would like to be addressed.

It's almost always best to address clients or customers by *Mr.* or *Ms.* until you are asked to do otherwise. The exception might be someone who is close to your own age.

Lynn recalls, "There was this wonderful woman in my company. I swear she got along with every person—there were about two hundred of us—in that building. She didn't have a mean bone in her body. Of course, it's impossible to get along with everyone. She *had* to be acting with some people, but you'd never be able to tell. I often think of her and wish I could be more like that. The message here is, always try to get along."

Be sure to show your boss and coworkers consideration and respect. Stop what you're doing when someone enters your office or work area and give that person your full attention. If your phone rings while you're speaking with someone in your work area, you can either answer it and quickly explain you're in a meeting and will call back soon, or let it go to your voice mail. Your choice will depend on your company's emphasis on answering every phone call personally, as well as on the importance of the meeting you are having. You may also be expected to answer your neighbors' phones if they are away from their desks; find out for sure before you let their calls go to a secretary or voice mail.

Office etiquette also covers little things like making a fresh pot of coffee if you've just poured yourself the last cup; contributing promptly to the coffee fund; helping to keep the kitchen area clean (and remembering to toss out your slightly furry sandwich from the refrigerator); not reading a coworker's mail; not borrowing desk items without asking first; and avoiding a host of other actions that would drive you nuts if they happened to you.

Phone Etiquette. Find out how your company wants you to answer the phone. If you're the first person the caller talks to, you'll probably want to answer with something like, "Good morning, XYZ Company. Roger speaking." If the call goes through a receptionist or secretary first, a simpler "Roger Jones" or "This is Roger Jones" is usually sufficient.

Learn the complexities of your phone system—like how to forward calls and how to transfer the caller to a voice mail box— in those first few days on the job when you may be looking for things to do. Ask the secretary or receptionist for a lesson or two during his or her slow periods, and take good notes.

If you are asked to answer phones, either occasionally or as part of your job, do so without complaint. Try to help the callers as much as you can—they're usually customers, so how you treat them is especially important. Always ask, "May I tell him who is calling?" and take care to pronounce the name right. Also be meticulous when taking messages. No one will mind (they'll actually be impressed) if you take the time to get the name spelled right and the phone number verified.

Never respond to a question with "I don't know." Instead, tell the caller you'll try to find an answer or the right person for her to talk to. Then make sure you get back to the caller as soon as possible with the answer. Whatever you do, don't transfer the call to someone you *think* might know the answer. Once you're given a question or a problem to solve, make it yours until it's answered or resolved. Passing the buck will only earn you a bad reputation. If finding the answer will take more than a minute or so, say so and offer to call the person back. Always ask first before putting the caller on hold for more than a minute.

If the caller makes an unusual request of you or your company, don't automatically say, "No, we don't do that." Instead, say, "I'm not sure—let me find out and get back to you." Even if the answer is still no, the customer will feel that you tried.

Voice Mail Etiquette. Voice mail is commonplace these days, and although it has its benefits, many people feel it can be a barrier to getting things done. Some people seem never to answer their phones directly, preferring to let all calls go to voice mail. You'll hear the term *telephone tag* used to describe the problem of never being able to reach the person you need to talk to, a problem that can delay projects and tasks for days on end. If you must leave a message, give as much information about your question or problem as you can, so that the person you're calling can leave *you* a voice mail message that provides the answer.

People who are genuinely busy find voice mail to be a valuable tool. But in your first year on the job, you should try to answer your phone whenever possible. Your boss and coworkers may feel that your entry-level position does not justify extensive use of this technology just yet, and they may think you're using voice mail to avoid picking up the phone.

You should also get in the habit of returning all your calls, and returning them promptly—the same day if possible. If people have to call a second or third time to get what they need from you, they will quickly label you as unreliable and unhelpful. You'll be surprised how fast this opinion will get back to your boss.

Here are a few other tips for using voice mail effectively:

• Don't eat or drink while leaving a message—it sounds terrible to the person on the other end of the line.

• Before you pick up the phone, prepare in your mind what you'll say if you have to leave a message. Don't be fumbling around looking for notes, numbers, and other vital information while you're recording your message.

• Identify yourself completely and mention the time and day you called—don't just say, "This is John." Even if your first name is not that common, it's more professional to say, "This is John Jones from XYZ Corporation returning your call. It's nine o'clock Thursday morning." Many voice mail systems allow users to check the time of the message, but it's helpful to get in the habit of stating the time you called. You may also want to mention a good time to reach you at your desk.

• Try not to leave excessively long messages—one minute should be the maximum. Get to the point quickly, without a lot of rambling.

• Always speak slowly when you leave your return phone number. Most people whiz through it—after all, they know it well, but all the listener hears is a blur of numbers.

LEARNING TO DO YOUR JOB

Don't be surprised if you feel a bit overwhelmed by your job at first. Everyone does, whether it's the first job or the fifth. Remember, in your first few weeks your boss realizes that you need some training and guidance, so your primary goal during that time is to try to absorb and learn, not to produce record-breaking results.

Learning at work is quite different from learning at school. You won't have textbooks to study and refer to, and you won't be listening to lectures. At work, much of what you learn will be up to you and your ability to listen well, ask questions, take notes, and observe others. The more you take the initiative in this process, the better off you will be.

Your boss or a coworker will probably sit down with you during those first few days and explain the details of how to perform the various parts of your job. Take plenty of notes so you'll have something to refer to, and don't be afraid to ask questions about anything you don't understand.

If it seems as if people are constantly at your side, telling you what to do during these first few days and weeks, don't think

Rick, a computer technician, recalls, "I was teaching a new guy how to carry out a lengthy operation, and I noticed he wasn't taking notes. I told him it would be a good idea to do so, but he brushed me off. I knew he'd be coming back later to ask me to repeat things. Always take notes when you're learning something new, and refer to them before going back to the person with questions. You'll learn a lot faster that way."

that they don't trust you. Your "coaches" will be back to their own jobs soon enough, and there'll be times when you wish they were around to help you out. If you show that you appreciate their help now, you can count on it later when you need them again.

During these first few weeks, you'll probably feel like a prisoner, even if you had full-time summer jobs while you were in school. The difference is that you knew those jobs were temporary and would end in two or three months. But this job, especially around four o'clock in the afternoon, seems to stretch endlessly into the future. Get out of the office for lunch whenever you can; you'll be surprised how it will break up the day and refresh you for the afternoon ahead. In a few months, when you're a working part of the team and have lots to do, the day will fly by. For now, just work on getting through it.

Get Technically Competent

You may be expected to learn new computer software. If so, do whatever it takes to get up to speed, even if it means spending your own time to work through a printed or on-line tutorial. Some companies will send new employees to training classes, but don't count on it. Learning new programs is simply a business fact of life these days, and companies usually expect the employee to take the initiative.

Learn to operate office equipment as well. In today's businesses, even high-level managers often make their own copies and send their own faxes. Get a lesson on the functions and capabilities of the photocopier. Learn how to fix paper jams and other minor problems so you don't find yourself alone with a balky copier late one night, trying to get copies made for an early-morning meeting. If you run into a problem you can't fix, don't simply abandon the machine without alerting the person who is responsible for its repair. (If you're really conscientious, you'll also post a note on the machine saying it's out of order and that the problem has been reported.)

Learn More About the Company

Make the most of any extra time you may have in these early days. Read your company's policies and procedures manual (if it has one) very carefully and start a list of questions about anything you don't understand. Be especially sure you understand benefits such as health insurance, leave policy, the 401(k) plan, holidays, overtime and compensatory time policies, and so on. It's your personal responsibility to know these things, and you may discover that your company won't be very understanding if you forget to sign up for insurance in time or misread the policy on personal time off.

During your first few days, go through any files, reports, manuals, or books that were left behind by your predecessor. Everything will be foreign to you at this point, so don't be too concerned if it all seems a bit overwhelming. At least you can start to get an idea of what you'll be doing, and names and terms won't sound quite so strange when your boss mentions them later.

Ask the secretary or administrative assistant for reading materials that might help you learn more about the company or your job. You might ask for the user's manuals for your phone system and computer software, for example, or back issues of the company newsletter.

If you didn't research your company's history and products or services before you took the job, now is the time to do so. On your own time, go to the public library (or your corporate library if there is one) to get a better idea of the larger world you are now a part of. If nothing else, you will see better how you fit into the big picture, and you will also be able to ask more intelligent questions. If your library search doesn't produce much, ask questions at work. Most people will be impressed that you want to know.

While you're learning about the company, ask to see a copy of an organization chart. Find out what other people do and what their titles really mean. This will help you put your work and your department in perspective. For example, it's a long-standing joke in most companies that a title like "Manager, Special Projects" sounds impressive but really means "we like the guy and he used to be valuable, but for various reasons we needed to move him out of the way." Nowadays, it's just as likely that the company has offered such a person an attractive severance or retirement package, but jobs like this are still around.

Also try to learn more about the person your boss reports to and what that person is like. Keep in mind that when your boss comes to you with a request or complaint, he may be responding to a request or complaint his own boss made. Over time, you'll learn more about this person, her importance in the company, and her priorities and values; for now, ask a few questions and keep your eyes and ears open.

The first few months are the best time to get organized and learn how to manage your time and your workload. Chapter 6, Getting the Job Done, describes techniques and approaches that will help you work efficiently and meet deadlines.

Know What's Expected of You

Probably the most important thing you can learn in these first few weeks is to find out exactly what is expected of you. This may be harder than it sounds. For example, say that part of your job involves taking orders from customers. You figure that as long as you get complete and accurate information, you've done a good job. But your boss may be expecting that you will try to soft-sell the customer on other company products or services as well, and that you will be chatty and friendly with the customer, not cool and detached.

For example, one of Lisa's customers, who was accustomed to superfriendly treatment from other employees, complained to Lisa's boss that she was cold and unhelpful. Lisa's boss was not happy and told Lisa so. The sad part was that Lisa truly thought she was doing a good job. Her mistake was not knowing what her boss really expected of her. In this case, Lisa might have prevented the problem by asking her boss to listen in on a customer phone conversation or go with her on her first visit to a customer. Ideally, your boss would suggest this approach, but many managers take things for granted. You may have to look out for yourself when it comes to learning more about your boss's unspoken expectations.

Another good way to learn what's important to your boss is to ask questions about the person who had your job before you. If the person was fired or transferred, try to determine why (you may need to ask your coworkers some discreet questions). For example, if your predecessor was a pushover when customers made unreasonable demands, and his actions cost the company money, you'll know that you'd better be able to stand firm when necessary. It's a safe bet that your boss will be watching for the same weakness in you.

In summary, to learn what is expected of you, do two basic things: Ask lots of questions and observe the behavior and the successes and failures of your coworkers. And don't assume anything. If you're not sure, ask.

Sweat the Small Stuff

The next challenge is to pay attention to the details of your job. You may have seen the T-shirt that reads, "Don't sweat the small stuff" on the front; the back reads, "It's all small stuff." Remember the second sentence. Even if you wow customers and management with superb customer service skills, you'll still be in trouble if your orders have errors in them or don't get processed on time.

Make sure you understand priorities as well. For example, one of Sean's jobs was to prepare a monthly inventory report, due no later than the fifth of the following month. Sean assumed, correctly so, that the report was used by management to monitor sales and determine when to reorder. In this department, dollar sales were cited in another report and reordering of these products occurred quarterly. It seemed to Sean that if things were busy, he could put off doing the report. As a result, every few months or so he turned in the report a week or more late, and then only after his boss had reminded him to get it done.

What Sean failed to realize was that the accounting department needed this report to complete each month's corporate financial statements. If he had asked questions to get a better picture of the report's importance—or simply delivered the report on time, as he had been instructed to do—he wouldn't have made this mistake. Unfortunately, his lack of concern led to a negative statement on his yearly performance appraisal.

At this point, you're probably asking, "Well, what really counts? Is it getting the details right, figuring out what my boss really wants, or having a positive attitude and taking a lot of initiative?" The answer is, it all really counts. But if you can't conquer the small stuff, nothing else will matter.

> Bill, a junior accountant in a large consulting firm, notes, "I find that when you overlook the details, that's the one time your boss asks for them. Then you feel like you weren't completely prepared. Overlooking the details seems to be a big negative among bosses."

Take Grunt Work Seriously

Like it or not, you'll have plenty of opportunity to prove you can do the small stuff. You'll be given plenty of it, since you're the new kid on the block (excuse the expression, but that is indeed how you will be viewed, even if you graduated summa cum laude from a very good school). In your first few months, in fact, you most likely will be asking yourself why you went to college (be sure to say this to yourself, not out loud). In fact, at this point you figure you could have done this job after graduating from middle school.

Here's how to cope with getting stuck with the grunt work: Take it in stride, take it as a challenge, and take it as a test.

The way you go about completing grunt work will tell your

boss and your coworkers a lot about you. Are you a complainer? Do you procrastinate? Do you think you are better than they are because of your strong academic credentials or social standing? Do you care about getting even the little things done right, regardless of their seeming unimportance to the overall operation? Think about it.

If you take the grunt work in stride, and also do it extremely well, you'll make a positive first impression. You'll come across as someone who is willing to start at the bottom (as almost everyone did at one time), someone who is a team player, and someone who cares about the details. None of this will hurt you as you move up in the company. Once you've proven yourself on these seemingly unimportant tasks, your boss will be much more likely to give you more challenging assignments. But first she needs to see your basic strengths and weaknesses.

If you really want to make a good impression, *volunteer* to do grunt work.

Own Up to Your Mistakes

Accept the fact that no matter how hard you try, you will make mistakes in your first few months on the job. In fact, you will make mistakes throughout your entire career—everyone does. You've probably heard this advice before, but remember that it's the way you handle your mistakes that counts.

First, admit to any mistakes you make, even the smallest ones. If you try to cover them up, downplay them, make excuses, or blame someone else, you'll come across as immature and unprofessional and perhaps a little dishonest. The best thing to do is admit the mistake, apologize if necessary, and get to work to repair the damage.

Some people are so afraid of making mistakes that they take forever to finish a job (and miss important deadlines) and take few or no risks. In these early weeks, you won't be doing too much risk taking, but you will be developing an approach to mistakes that will help you cope with errors in timing or judgment down the road. Accept the fact that no one is perfect and understand that your worth as an employee and a human being is not at stake over a miscalculation or a missed opportunity. Mistakes always have a positive side: They usually teach us something, whether it's learning to double-check our math or seeing the need for better sales skills. The proverb that says we learn more from our failures than we do from our successes states a basic fact of life, both business and personal.

> Paige confesses, "If I make a mistake that was due to carelessness, I say to myself, 'I'll never let that happen again.' Then I hold myself to that promise. Just stating the problem seems to help keep me from repeating it."

Keep a Low Profile

As mentioned earlier, don't spend the first few months on your first job—or on any other job you'll ever have, for that matter—trying to act like you know it all. On the contrary, try to lie low and absorb all you can for a while. Unless you see something simple and fairly obvious that needs fixing, don't make suggestions on how to improve things until you completely understand the operation yourself—which could take months. Until you can say for sure otherwise, assume that there is a good reason things are done the way they are—for now, anyway.

THE PROBATIONARY PERIOD

Some companies will tell you that your first three months on the job are probationary and that your performance will be evaluated at the end of that period. Others will not have a formal probationary period, but you can be sure that your work and actions will be watched closely during that time. In these crucial early weeks, you should be aware of a few things.

First, your boss really wants you to do well because your performance will reflect on him as a manager. He selected you as the best from among many qualified candidates, and it's important to him personally and to his corporate reputation to have made a good choice. You can also be sure that he would rather not go through the hiring process again anytime soon. In short, you will really have to disappoint him to get fired at this point.

However, if he or others see problems with your work or your behavior that they think do not bode well for the future, they may decide to cut their losses early on. Whether they take action this soon depends on the company's culture and personnel policies. This is why making a good impression during those first few weeks is so important.

If you're lucky, your boss will give you a formal evaluation at the end of the probationary period. You may not like the idea of hearing about any shortcomings so early in the game, but it will be much easier to fix problems now rather than risk compounding them as your time on the job increases (and when your boss and coworkers won't be quite as forgiving as they were when you were new).

Most managers dread giving negative feedback, however, and you may have to find the courage to simply ask, "How do you think I am doing? Is there anything you'd like me to do differently?" If your boss comes back with a vague or general comment or two, ask her for examples—and make sure you understand the problem. Try to listen to these comments without being defensive or hurt. And whatever you do, don't argue, criticize, or complain; simply listen and then think for a day or two about what she said. If things are truly not as your boss sees them, discuss it with her later, when you can do so in an unemotional way.

To put criticism in perspective, try to remember that everything you're doing is a learning experience at this point, and your goal is to conquer the basics of your job so you can prepare to move up.

If you rarely receive positive feedback, don't get depressed.

Your boss is probably the type who takes good work for granted and saves praise for work that goes above and beyond your job description. Most managers take this approach, usually unintentionally. In fact, it's usually safe to assume that you are doing a good job unless you hear otherwise. This is just another way that work is different from school—don't expect comments on everything you turn in. But be assured that if you are doing a good job, it's being noticed and appreciated.

SUMMARY

The way you come across in your first few weeks on the job will stay in people's minds for a long time. You'll do fine if you keep these thoughts in mind:

• You may have learned a lot in school and be eager to apply it right away, but hold off. You'll learn more about business and your chosen field in the next six months than you learned about it in four years of college. Keep an open mind and keep learning.

• Be aware of how you look, act, and speak. This is not the time to make a fashion statement or act as if you're still a student who doesn't want to face the real world. You will be treated as an equal if you present yourself as an adult.

• Ask questions freely and listen carefully to the answers. In general, listen more than talk.

• Don't be afraid to make mistakes, and don't be afraid to ask for feedback. The more you can learn now, the easier your job will be later.

• Don't take criticism—or the lack of praise—personally. View your first job as a postgraduate learning experience, not as a judgment on your value as a human being.

• Watch your attitude. It will show, even when you think you are keeping your thoughts to yourself. The next chapter explains why attitude is so important to your success.

2

Why Attitude Matters Most

You've recently completed sixteen or seventeen years of school, and you're feeling pretty good about it. In fact, it's hard to believe that this part of your life has come to an end. But you made it, and you're pleased with yourself. You're on top of the world, and even the thought of finding a job didn't trouble you.

But once you started the job, reality set in. The fact that you were a class leader, honors student, or your parents' pride and joy no longer seems to matter. In an instant, you're at the bottom rung of the ladder, with no power and no glory. Everything is new and strange, you probably don't know anybody, and it hits you that you will have to prove yourself all over again.

But wait. It's not as bad as it seems. For one thing, everyone has to start somewhere; even Bill Gates had to learn how to write computer code. For another, you should realize that your new boss understands that she has to invest a lot in your training in the first year or two. She's not expecting that you'll be able to learn everything right away—although she'll be pleased if you're enthusiastic and a fast learner.

You'll be surprised at how much you'll have to learn, and even more surprised to find out that very little of what you learned in school—even if your job is in the same field as your college major—will help you in your day-to-day tasks. Why, then, did you go to college? You've probably heard it before: to prove to your future employers that you had the persistence and smarts to stick with something tough. They'd also like to know that you learned to read and write well, but a college degree is not necessarily proof of those skills.

You'll also come to see that the strengths you need to succeed at work are different from those that helped you succeed in school, with the exception of basic intelligence and the ability to persevere mentioned above. At school, much of your success depended on good study habits and the ability to take tests well. At work, you'll neither study nor take tests. But you will be tested in a different way—not only for your skills in getting the job done but on the way you work with and get along with your boss and other people. If your kindergarten teacher wrote, "Plays well with others" on your report card, you may have an edge in the real world.

In his best-selling book, *Emotional Intelligence*, Daniel Goleman mentions a study that followed the progress of eighty-one valedictorians and salutatorians from the class of 1981 in Illinois high schools. "But while they continued to achieve well in college, getting excellent grades, by their late twenties they had climbed to only average levels of success. Ten years after graduating from high school, only one in four was at the highest level of young people of comparable age in their chosen professions, and many were doing much less well."

The single most important factor in your success on the job, both now and in the future, is your *attitude*. Of course we mean a *positive* attitude, but it's really more than that. Your attitudes reveal to those around you your innermost thoughts and beliefs about people and situations. In your first year on the job, people will be watching your attitude closely.

Consider the difference in attitude between Laura and Dana. They were recently hired for identical positions. When Dana is assigned a task, the first thing she does is to complain to anyone who will listen how difficult it is and how much work she'll have to do to get it done. Laura, given the same task, has similar concerns but sets her mind to getting the work done, keeping her thoughts to herself. Both workers will complete the task successfully, but Laura will come across as the more capable employee.

Attitude is conveyed in many different ways, some obvious and some hidden. It's when your negative attitude is obvious to others and hidden to you that problems arise. The following examples are typical negative attitudes heard or otherwise experienced by people in their first job. If you hear yourself even *thinking* any of these statements, stop and consider how they might be interpreted by others.

CAREER-KILLING STATEMENTS

"I'm too busy [i.e., important] to do that—give it to the secretary."
The attitude that this thought conveys can be deadly in your first year on the job. You're really saying several things. First, if you think a task is beneath you and you give it to one of the support staff, you're taking the chance that you'll be seen as someone who doesn't take direction well; "disobeys orders" is a stronger way of putting it. Yes, the task may be grunt work, but perhaps your boss wanted you to learn a process from the bottom up, which is often the best way to learn.

Second, you'll be seen by your coworkers as smug and self-important and by the support staff as—face it—a spoiled brat. If you think mailroom clerks, copy machine operators, and secretaries aren't important to your success, you're vastly underestimating how much they can help you, especially when you're in a pinch.

Later on, you'll learn that delegating tasks is key to getting your job done. For now, do them yourself unless you're told otherwise. If you truly need help, check with your boss before you reassign any work.

"Don't bother me with the details—
I'm more concerned with the big picture."

This attitude is similar to the one just discussed, with an emphasis on misplaced self-importance. You simply have not been on the job long enough to be this important. The only person who can get away with this statement is the president or the CEO, and chances are any top executive will still want the details before making a decision.

In addition, you'll be revealing your ignorance of the basic business fact that the big picture is usually gained only after close examination of many small details. For example, a monthly sales report—used to give an overall view of progress for the month—consists of many relevant details in addition to bottom-line dollar sales. The report gives information such as which geographic regions had the most sales, which products or services did well and which didn't, which salespersons did well and which didn't, and so on. The "big picture" may be that product A continues to lag in sales in the western states. To solve the problem revealed by the big picture, management will have to examine the details. After much investigation, these managers may find they have an unmotivated salesperson in that region who has shown little interest in pushing a new product because the employee doesn't understand how it works. It might take a great deal of persistence and detail work to figure out a problem like this one, but the solution may be as simple as sending the salesperson to special training on the product.

Robert worked in a department whose director had a habit of dropping by unannounced and asking, "How are things going?" Robert was savvy enough to know he wasn't expected to answer with a simple "Fine." He knew the director was really saying, "I'd like to know what you're working on—give me an overview and some pertinent details." Robert replied, "Do you have a moment?" and then pulled out sales reports and explained not only what progress had been made but a few reasons why. Often these unplanned, unrehearsed opportunities to show others your abilities turn out to be the most crucial moments of your career.

"Nobody told me to (so I didn't)."

The attitude this statement can convey (depending on the circumstances and how the words are spoken) is "Hey, I'll do anything anyone asks me to do, but don't expect me to do one more thing." In your first few weeks, you'll be able to plead ignorance, but once you know more about the job, you'll be expected to do it completely whether or not you are asked. To do otherwise is to give the impression that you are dense, uncooperative, and there only to take orders and collect a paycheck. In some companies, this is known as having an "hourly mentality," referring to lower-level employees who are paid by the hour and have no real commitment to the job or the company.

This statement is often used as an excuse. If you were not aware that you were supposed to do something but your boss feels you should have been, it's best to simply say, "I'm sorry. I'll be sure to do it next time."

"I couldn't finish on time because no one would help me."

This statement sends two messages: You weren't smart enough to ask for help earlier, when it might have been granted, and you tend to whine. As an excuse, it's pretty weak. You would never have tried it on your economics professor, and it certainly won't work with your boss.

In fact, you may have a good reason for not finishing on time. The deadline may have been unrealistic from the start (no one took into account your newness to the job) or may have been based on an inadequate initial estimate of the time needed. You may have been given other projects in the meantime, and your time management and juggling skills still need development. Someone may have been assigned to help you but then failed to show up, and you decided to try to do it yourself rather than complain.

To avoid this kind of problem in the first place, learn to speak up early on. Let your boss know of any barriers you're facing, whether it's the demands of other projects, lack of cooperation from coworkers, or simply your inexperience at handling multiple tasks. If you sound an alarm early enough, your boss will be concerned but glad there's still time to make the deadline. If you wait too long, you risk missing the deadline and getting your boss in trouble as well, and that's not good.

"Don't blame me—I hardly had anything to do with it."
When you say this to your boss, there's a good chance he's looking at you and seeing visions of his six-year-old son who just broke a living room lamp and is trying to implicate his younger sister. If you start to remind your boss of his children, you're in trouble. Don't expect to move up the ladder anytime soon, if at all.

Statements like this one reveal a lot about a person's maturity and integrity. It may be tough to confess your mistakes, but you shouldn't hesitate. Do it quickly, apologize if necessary, learn something from the mistake, and move on. There's usually no need to fall on your sword and make a big deal out of the goof; in fact, overreaction is almost as undesirable as denying responsibility. Everyone makes mistakes, even your boss, and he will know how hard it is for you to come forth. He'll respect you for it.

"I'll offer my ideas when they pay me more."
Earlier we told you to hold off on giving advice and solving major business problems until you have been on the job long enough— probably at least six months—to figure out what is really going on. But some employees feel that because their pay is relatively low, they should hold back on offering any ideas that might save the company time or money or bring new business its way.

The problem with this attitude is that it can turn around and bite you. You'll miss out on establishing yourself as someone who even *has* ideas. While you're waiting to be paid enough, you're risking being passed over for promotion—because you seemingly have nothing more to offer than your daily presence on the job.

A good idea is valued highly in most companies, small and large. If you're doing a fair amount of grunt work—which you probably are at this point—you are in a great place to see ineffi-ciencies, duplications, and easier and faster ways to get things done. Many procedures that seem set in stone are really just ways of doing things that someone set up years ago, when personal computers were nonexistent and business processes were quite different from today. After you've been on the job a few months and fully understand what you're doing and the reasons why, step back and give the process a critical look. Chances are you'll see a few places where things could be done better. Mention these to your boss—ideally in a memo—and explain the value of your suggestions and how they could be implemented.

If you have ideas that you think might benefit your group as a whole, run them by your coworkers—and don't worry about not getting full credit if the idea is used. Your idea may be sound but need fine-tuning by people who have more experience than you do, or it may trigger an even better idea. Sharing your ideas freely and recognizing that you don't necessarily have all the answers will establish you as a valuable member of the team. You'll also be developing solid working relationships that will pay off later on.

Whatever you do, don't hoard good ideas. It could cost you in the long run.

"No one will notice if I let this slide for a while."
Yes, they will, sooner or later. Either way, you'll risk being labeled a procrastinator and disorganized as well. The biggest problem with letting things slide is that sometimes they slide

away completely—and you forget about them. Then one day your boss asks you where you filed the Jones report, and you have to answer that you haven't filed it yet. In fact, you haven't even completed it yet. Oops.

"This is harder than I thought it would be—I'll get back to it later."
Closely related to the previous statement, this attitude reflects procrastination in its purest form. We all want to do the easy tasks first and avoid those we're afraid we'll fail at. If you can make yourself do it, though, tackling the difficult tasks first makes the rest of your job easy. Don't be afraid to ask for help or advice. Most managers understand that you're new, and they will be glad to explain further, or even to explain a second time. What they *won't* understand is an assignment done late, done incorrectly, or not done at all.

"It's not in my job description."
If your boss or someone else in authority asks you to complete a task that is not normally part of your job, do it happily. If you balk or whine, you will encourage your boss and others never to ask you to do something extra again. In fact, they'll be saying to themselves, "Okay, it looks like Jennifer wants to stay right where she is." If two years from now you're complaining that you haven't been considered for promotion, don't be surprised. Besides, most job descriptions end with a clause that covers these requests: "Other duties as assigned."

Being flexible is one of the most important traits you can have. Very few things are black and white or always work the same way; change is part of today's business world. If you can adapt and go with the flow, you'll be ahead of a lot of other people.

Look at these "extra" assignments as a chance to prove that you can handle whatever your boss wants to throw at you. Accept these tasks enthusiastically, and you'll be showing your boss that you are ready for a promotion later on. The only time to voice concern is if you truly feel you can't get everything done on schedule. If that's the case, let your boss know how much you'd like to do the new task but mention that you may need her help in setting priorities.

"I'm sorry but I don't know the answer. Good-bye."

Most likely you'll be hearing the term *customer-service oriented* in the course of your job. One of the things this means is that all employees are expected to help the customer (and that usually includes "internal" customers, such as people in other departments) in any way possible. For example, if someone comes by or calls with a question that you can't answer, you should try to find the answer or the right person to ask. Make a few phone calls, or check with your boss or coworkers. But don't brush the person off. Your attitude will come back to haunt you.

"I didn't know you needed it so soon."

This statement is the twin of the attitude "It's not my responsibility to know anything more than I'm told." When your boss asks you to do something, it's up to you to think the task through and clarify anything you don't understand. For example, one of the most important parts of any assignment is its deadline. If your boss forgets to mention it, or is vague about it, ask for a date and time. If you want to be seen as a capable, responsible adult, take on some of the burden of getting all the facts you need.

"Sorry I can't help you with that—I'm just too busy."

Sometimes it's okay to say this—it shows that you are being responsible for your own work. But if you say this frequently to coworkers who are in a pinch (and they suspect you're really not that busy), you'll quickly earn a reputation for not being a team player. Down the road, when *you* need help to get something done on time, you'll find that everyone is too busy to help you. Remember the nursery story about the little red hen?

"I can't work late tonight—I have softball practice."

There is an unspoken belief among most managers that their employees will be available to work anytime they are needed, even on short notice. Your boss may not have mentioned this at your interview or your orientation, but you can be sure that if something has to get done by a certain time, you will be expected to stay to help out.

However, very few managers will actually demand that you stay late or work on the weekend—instead, they'll put it in the form of a request. Don't make the mistake of thinking you have an option. If you truly have something going on that is as important as your job—a serious family illness, your wedding, or perhaps even a trip with a nonrefundable deposit at stake—you might get away with saying no.

Most managers will not think that softball practice is more important than keeping or winning a major client, however. If you really must say no, it's often better not to give an excuse at all, just in case it appears to be as weak as this one.

On the other hand, you don't want to get yourself into a situation in which you are working so much overtime that your life is not your own. You also don't want to be the only person left working late every night. It's one thing to be cooperative and helpful, but it's another to be taken advantage of. If this type of situation continues, talk with your boss about it. If that doesn't work, you may want to start looking for another job.

Many companies have times of year when they are extremely busy. Try to find out if you are in one of those cycles, especially if you find yourself consistently working late. Just remember that most companies will expect you to put in extra hours from time to time. Be as cheerful as you can about it; a positive attitude will pay off later.

"I won't be in today. I have this terrible headache."
There are a lot of problems with this excuse, so be careful. First, remember that in your early months on the job, your boss will be more in tune than she'll ever be about your absences. If she's like most managers, she's been burned in the past by employees who abused sick leave in one way or another. Right now, she'll be sensitive to isolated problems that could predict major bad habits.

Second, the headache just might go away by noon (unless you're prone to daylong migraines). If you say you need the whole day off, you will invite skepticism about the true reason for your absence. You certainly don't want to appear to be untrustworthy at this point in your career. You might say you'll try to be in later and then set a time to call back and let your boss know if you will.

Third, if you call in sick too often, no matter what the excuse, you'll soon generate ill will among your coworkers. After all, they will have to do your work for you while you're out. No one minds helping out every once in a while, but if it's always for the same person, people naturally start feeling used and resentful. They'll also be watching closely to see how your manager handles the situation. If she ignores your frequent absences (and a few bosses will), your coworkers will come to resent her for being so unfair. Sooner or later, she'll have a morale problem on her hands, and it won't take her long to figure out the cause. If it's you, watch out.

If you're truly sick, however, don't come in. People don't want you to spread germs if you've got something infectious, and you probably won't be that productive anyway. The bottom line is to use sick leave judiciously and to remember that your boss will probably know (and understand) when you're really ill. Your coworkers may be getting away with taking an occasional "mental health" day, but you're too new even to think about doing that yet.

"Why should I learn that word processing program?
Isn't that what the secretary's for?"

If your office has a secretary, you're in luck. And if it does, that employee is probably responsible for more important things than typing your monthly report. In the past few years, most workers, even managers, have begun to do their own typing of internal documents. This makes sense because they're often composing their thoughts directly on the computer, not in longhand on a legal pad. As a result, many secretarial positions have been abolished, and those that are left have more substantive duties.

The main problem with this career-killing statement is that you come across as thinking you're too good, or too highly educated, or too well paid (unlikely) to lower yourself to such a task. If you say this to your boss, he'll be annoyed but perhaps slightly amused at your arrogance. If you say it in front of the secretary, you'll come to regret the remark for as long as you work there.

This situation recalls an earlier fact of work life: If your boss asks you to do something, do it, and do it cheerfully. That's why you were hired.

"I need an assistant."

This statement is related to the previous one. You may feel like saying this to your boss after a few weeks or months of doing monotonous work that you'd love to palm off on someone else. In this case, hold off. Patience is key.

You must realize that, in effect, you *are* the assistant at the moment. As we explained in Chapter 1, you are being tested in your first few months to see if you'll be ready to handle tougher assignments. Your boss is also watching for the attitudes discussed in this chapter, to make sure she's hired someone who will be a team player. If you ask for extra help in the form of a new staff person, your boss will think (1) you can't handle the manageable task load she thinks she's given you, (2) you've got a grander view of yourself than is called for by your position, or (3) you don't understand the business expense of hiring a permanent employee, no matter how low paid.

The best approach is to do the job the best you can, and within six months or a year you'll probably be given higher-level work. Most managers love to reward strong performers, because bosses know that good people will leave if they're not kept challenged. If you're still doing the same work two or three years down the road, you should probably start looking for another job (see more about this in Chapter 9).

You should also be aware that adding staff is done very cautiously in most companies these days. It can take months of formal justifications and documentation for a department to get approval for an additional full-time position.

"When will I be promoted?"

Unless your job is part of some formal program that spells out events like promotions, your boss may not be able to answer this question. If you ask it before the end of the first year, you will be revealing your expectation that promotions are automatic and based on time in the job. This is rarely the case anymore. Most promotions are given based on work quality, ability to work with others, and a positive attitude. In addition, an opening must be available. In today's tightly run companies, you may have to wait for someone to move up or out before you can be promoted. In some cases, however, your boss may be able to redefine the duties of your current job and persuade Human Resources to reevaluate it to justify a different title and a higher salary (see Chapter 8 for more about promotions and raises).

This question also may come across as presumptuous—it says that you fully expect to be promoted and that it's your boss's job to make a promotion happen. A better way to get the answer you need is to ask, "Exactly what will I need to accomplish to be considered for a promotion?"

CAREER-BUILDING ATTITUDES

Here are a few words that the people around you will love to hear. They mean a lot because they reflect a commitment to the job and to the organization. Words like these will speak volumes about the kind of person you are:

- "Sure, I'll take care of it. When do you need it?"
- "Would you like me to do that as well?"
- "Don't worry—I'll stay until it's done."
- "I've got a little downtime. Can I help you with anything?"

WHEN UNSPOKEN THOUGHTS SPEAK VOLUMES

Your attitudes come across just as loudly by the way you act as by the words you say. Your facial expressions, your body language, and your tone of voice all give away your innermost thoughts, whether good or bad. In fact, a rule of thumb among communications researchers is that 90 percent of an emotional message is nonverbal.

This is not to say you have to smile all the time or never have a bad day. But you should realize that people are pretty good at sensing your true thoughts. For example, if you frown and shake your head as your boss explains your latest assignment, she will know that you are not keen on doing it—you don't have to say a word. And even if you do say positive things about the task, your tone of voice will probably give your thoughts away. The scary thing is that you may not be aware of how you're coming across. Try to become more attuned to the physical expressions you may be showing. Read Julius Fast's book *Body Language in the Work Place*—it's a fascinating description of how to learn to read other people and to avoid giving away your inner thoughts.

A POSITIVE ATTITUDE IS MADE, NOT BORN

Do you find yourself thinking or voicing many of the statements listed earlier in this chapter? If so, you should seriously examine your overall attitude toward work itself. Do you view work as a basic and potentially rewarding part of life, both personal and professional? Or is your job just a way to gain power, make lots of money, and impress all those people you went to school with?

People who enjoy what they do tend to define success as achieving certain inner goals—the joy of doing a job well, of being part of a winning team, of taking on and conquering new challenges. To them, monetary reward, power, and recognition are side benefits, not the primary motivation. These are the people who are most successful in the long run, by any standard.

If you think that some people are just born with a positive outlook, you're probably partly right. But we can all control our reactions and attitudes toward the world around us, even when we can't change the world itself.

The reality is that there is no perfect job, no perfect boss, no perfect place to work. You might find a terrific and caring boss, but the work is dull and boring. Or your company may be three blocks from your apartment, but the pay is lousy. Many young people jump from job to job in search of some ideal combination before they come to the conclusion that such jobs are extremely rare.

Here's where you have to accept reality and deal with it the best you can. For example, your boss rarely speaks to you, even though you were hoping that he would be your mentor—he's terrific at what he does. Your working conditions aren't great, and you're sharing a crowded cubicle with three other employees. Also, the commute is much worse than you thought it would be, and you're strung out by the time you arrive each day. The one saving grace is that you really like your work, even if it is entry-level. You know it will give you the foundation you need to move up. Nevertheless, when you tally up the pros and cons, the cons have it. Is it time to start sending out résumés?

We'll talk more in Chapter 9 about how to tell when it's time to leave a job, but for now let's look at the example in the preceding paragraph. Your commute is such a stressful experience that you start every day on the wrong foot. You probably don't realize it, but your antagonistic reaction to it is making some things at the office look worse than they really are. If there are no feasible alternatives for getting to work, you can face the fact that you can't control the traffic, but you can control your attitude toward it. You might say to yourself, "This is how it is, and I'm just not going to let it get to me anymore. I'm stronger than that. I'll use my time alone in the car to play tapes, think about what I'm going to accomplish that day, or just daydream. But cursing at the traffic is not doing me any good."

Other problems can be dealt with in a similar way. You can make a boring task more interesting by trying to find better or faster ways to do it, perhaps giving yourself a small reward each time you meet your goal. An editorial assistant whose job was to proofread financial tables day after day—a mind-numbing task if there ever was one—gave herself a small piece of candy for each error she found. Although this may sound like an approach used to train animals, it worked for her and helped keep her alert and motivated.

Although we've been stressing attitude in this chapter, mastering the technical aspects of your job should also be a goal in your first year. If you perform poorly or lackadaisically, you could be on the way out. If you perform well and with some enthusiasm, your boss will have evidence that you're ready for more challenges, perhaps even a promotion. This may sound overly simplistic, but it's usually what happens. Why should a manager promote someone who can't do an entry-level job well?

It may take months for your boss to notice how well you're doing, but don't let it get to you. She's got many other things to worry about, and she's probably spending much of her time dealing with problems. She may not say so, but for now she is very glad you're not one of her problems; it may take her a little longer to see your progress and accomplishments. In the meantime, praise yourself. The single most important job satisfaction tool you can develop is to take pride in your work, no matter what it is. It may sound corny, but if you can go home at the end of each day knowing you did your best, and knowing your work advanced the goals of the organization in some way, however small, you will feel good about yourself and your job.

It also helps to keep in mind that you will not be in this job forever, and that it is just the first in many steps toward a job that will offer other rewards as well.

A FINAL WORD ABOUT ATTITUDE

The next sentence may sound severe, but it's key to how you think about work. If you are expecting your boss or your company to take care of your needs and chart your career for you, you'll almost certainly be disappointed. You, in fact, were hired to take care of *their* needs, in a manner of speaking. If you start to think that they need you more than you need them, you may be in for a rude surprise one day. In corporate life, it's true that no one is irreplaceable. This sounds harsh, but it's a fact of business life, no matter how valuable we think our contributions are.

The reality is that you're not a kid anymore. At work in particular, people will be treating you like an adult, and they will expect you to act like one in return. The next chapter explains more about professional attitudes and behaviors at work.

3

Becoming a Professional

It's hard to believe that you're finally on your own. You've gained the freedom from parents and teachers that you've longed for—but soon you realize that your life is now partially controlled by your company and your boss. It's a fact of life that no matter how old you are, unless you're independently wealthy, other people will still have some degree of control over your life. The best thing to do is to accept the fact. If it really bothers you, strive to become a company president or run your own business.

One of the big differences between school and work is the amazing variety of people you'll have to deal with. Your boss might be old enough to be your grandfather or young enough to be your older sister. You'll work with people from all kinds of backgrounds and with all types of personalities, from relaxed and easygoing to tense and demanding. Your ultimate success in your first job and in any other job will depend on how well you work with all types of people, regardless of age, social class, position in the organization, or personality.

This does not mean you have to be Mr. or Ms. Congeniality, although frankly that wouldn't hurt. But it does mean that you need to develop a certain empathy for people and a basic understanding of why they behave as they do. This is primarily for your sake, not theirs.

You will also move ahead faster and gain the respect of your coworkers if you exhibit professional behavior right from the start. The following sections explain what we mean by *professional behavior.*

NO WHINING

Whining about your job, your personal life, your boss, or your finances is probably the single most irritating habit you could have. No one likes a whiner, and most offices already have their share.

After a couple of months on the job, Bob had completely alienated his office mate with his constant stream of pathetic complaints: "This job is for morons, and I don't see the point of all this paperwork." "Our boss is impossible—there's just no pleasing him." "I wish I could find the time to revise my résumé so I could get out of this place." You know the type—you'll go out of your way to avoid getting trapped listening to someone like this. But would you recognize this behavior in yourself? Pay attention to what you say. Try to catch yourself in the act. If you're aware of the problem, you'll be more likely to control it. This doesn't mean that you can't let off steam. Just try to do it with a good friend or family member, not with people at the office.

NO EXCUSES

If you fail to do something or if you do it incorrectly, the best thing to do is to apologize quickly and quietly and vow to yourself it won't happen again. You may have a perfectly good reason for the flub, but unless your excuse is pretty unusual, no one wants to hear it. Your manager and others will be more concerned about correcting the problem than in listening to you go into excruciating detail about why you did what you did.

In fact, the most professional thing you can do after you apologize is to correct the problem—immediately.

KNOWING WHEN TO KEEP YOUR MOUTH SHUT

Knowing when to speak up and when to stay silent is a skill that few people have mastered, but it's a great one to have. Most of us tend to say what's on our minds, then, later on, regret much of what we said. In an office there are several reasons to watch what you say and who you say it to.

Avoid Gossip

You'll be surprised how fast words travel in an office, especially words that are potentially embarrassing or damaging. Stacey had become fairly close to Jean, the receptionist, and they often had lunch together. One day Stacey confided in Jean that her car had been repossessed because she couldn't make the payments. Within a few days Stacey began receiving offers for rides to work from some of her coworkers, to her great embarrassment. Stacey hadn't worked there long enough to know that Jean was the office busybody and gossip, and in her front desk position, she was in a great place to spread the word. If you must share personal details in your first few months on the job, be sure you can trust the person you tell. Even better, say nothing at all to people at work, with the possible exception of your boss, who may need to know if something in your personal life will be affecting your work.

Wait a While

What you say in front of your superiors and coworkers may be held against you. Zack was eager to put his MBA knowledge to immediate good use. Within a few weeks of starting his job at a highly regarded software company, he was invited to attend a meeting his boss had called. Zack saw this meeting as a good opportunity to impress not only his boss but other managers with his ideas, some of which bore no relation to the topics at hand or the company's real needs. During the meeting, his boss was embarrassed (not to mention a little angry) and had to ask Zack to hold his discussion for another time. Later Zack was called into his boss's office and was read the riot act. It was months before Zack was invited to another meeting. The moral of this story is, don't offer your ideas until you've been around long enough to fully understand the problems at hand. If you wait, you'll be much more credible and your ideas will have a better chance of being accepted.

Don't Interrupt

If you have a question or comment to make while someone else is speaking, save it until the speaker is finished making his or her point. This piece of advice counts double when your boss or another manager is talking to you. Even in friendly conversations with coworkers, watch any tendencies you have to break into their stories with examples of your own—in other words, let people finish what they have to say. It's ironic, but good listeners are usually considered to be wonderful conversationalists.

Know When to Stop

In meetings and in conversations with your boss and others, get to the point quickly and stop. If you stretch out or embellish your ideas, ramble, repeat, or come off as unclear, you will lose the chance to make your point. People will simply shut you out. Think about what you plan to say before you say it. Pick the most salient points and emphasize them. If you're proposing an idea, have all your points and reasons well thought out and organized. Use as few words as possible, and make each word count.

Limit Chitchat

Pay attention to how much and how often you find yourself in office chitchat. It's easy to blow a few hours a day talking with coworkers about matters that don't relate to getting the job done. This also includes time spent reading and sending unnecessary E-mail. The biggest temptation will be to chat with your office mate or cubicle neighbor. Even if your boss is not located in the immediate area, all she has to do to form a negative impression of both of you is to drop in a few times while you're in animated conversation.

What if you're not the talker but your neighbor is? This can be a tricky situation, because you don't want to offend someone you have to spend eight hours a day with. Some people take a hint less readily than others, but you can try to say things like "I've got to get this done by four o'clock or else—talk with you later," or simply "Can't talk now." If the problem persists, you should let your boss know about it—you don't want to be wrongly implicated. It may be possible to rearrange your desk or to be moved to another location.

Here's a tip for discouraging drop-in visitors: If you happen to have an extra chair next to your desk where people tend to sit for a while, try stacking it with books and papers. If you really need to talk with someone—say, your boss comes in—you can quickly clear away the stack. Otherwise it can stay on the chair, sending a subtle but effective message.

The classic method for cutting short unwelcome visitors is to get up and start walking away, as if you've just remembered you're late for a meeting. If you can carry this off smoothly, the other person won't realize that he or she is being cut off. This technique often works where more subtle signals fail.

If you're the talker—and you are if people (1) start looking at their watches and saying they have to get back to work or (2) say, "Yes, you mentioned that earlier"—then try to control your urge to chat. Save long conversations for lunchtime and breaks.

This does not mean that you should strictly limit conversations with your boss and coworkers; friendly banter and small talk are essential elements of cooperation and understanding.

Watch Your Language

One good way *not* to act professionally is to use bad language. Some offices are more tolerant than others about this, but you can't go wrong by avoiding four-letter words, especially when you're not sure yet how they will be received. And like many other aspects of your personal behavior, people will not usually tell you to stop. Instead, they'll start to form a negative opinion of you, and you may never know exactly why you were passed over for promotion down the road.

Telling off-color jokes falls under this category as well. So do sexist, ageist, and racist remarks. You will never know whom you might offend, and it's just safer to refrain rather than to risk making enemies. You don't want people to form a negative opinion of you this early in the game. Even a seemingly innocent joke or remark can be interpreted differently by different people. Be careful.

Watch your speech also for excessive use of slang, especially the kind that will mark you as someone who was recently a teenager. You don't want your boss treating you like a kid, so try not to give the impression of being one.

Don't Overdo It

Do you tend to laugh too much or too loudly? Jim was a likable guy, but he had the irritating habit of laughing at just about anything he or anyone else said. When people noticed he laughed at bad news as well, they began to understand he was simply insecure. As it turned out, he had good reason to be insecure, because he had been hired for a job that was way over his head. He was fired within a year.

People tend to avoid those who laugh and talk too loudly. Like overactive talkers, they disrupt the office and are often the last to be considered for promotion, regardless of their skills.

Refrain from People Bashing

Here's a favorite office pastime—criticizing, making fun of, and otherwise bashing other people on the job. Once you get settled in, you will be surprised how much company time and energy is spent in tearing down others, coworkers and managers alike. It's easy to get dragged into one of these sessions, but they usually end up making you feel worse about your job and the organization, not better. Face it, you will not like 20 percent of the people you work with, and 20 percent will not like you, no matter what. The professional thing to do is to realize that no one is perfect and that some of your coworkers probably deserve to be criticized—but that doing so is not your responsibility and not an activity worthy of your time and energy.

Don't Be Rude

Good manners seem so basic, but you'd be surprised how many people forget to say "please" and "thank you" or even give a simple nod of the head when passing a coworker in the hall. The absence of these social graces translates to most people as rudeness. Of course, being really rude, as in letting doors slam on people behind you or failing to hold open the elevator door or performing countless other thoughtless acts, will soon brand you as a boor. Sarcastic comments seemingly meant in jest also usually come off as rudeness. The biggest act of rudeness of all, however, is failing to listen to what others are trying to say, as the next section explains.

LEARNING TO LISTEN

Most people are terrible listeners. We don't *really* listen to our friends, our spouses, our parents, our children, our bosses, or our coworkers. We may *think* we're listening, but chances are we've missed something because we've been too busy thinking about what we're going to say next. As a result, we miss out on important information, and we risk offending the speaker.

If you had to choose one interpersonal skill to work on in your first year on the job, pick listening. It will be the single most important tool you will ever have for getting along and getting ahead. Here's a brief rundown on how.

Give the Speaker Your Full Attention

Pay attention. This sounds so basic, and most of us think we are doing so. The problem is that your brain works so fast that it can easily handle two or three tasks at once. So while one part of your brain is listening to the speaker, another part is figuring out how to respond and yet another part has wandered off to something completely different, like what to have for dinner. Before you know it, you've missed something crucial that the speaker just said. If you're lucky enough to realize you've missed it, you can ask to have it repeated. Of course, then the speaker will know you haven't been listening, but it's better than the alternative—such as failing to do something asked of you.

The side benefit of giving your full attention is that the speaker is so gratified that you did. That person will be much more likely to give you a full hearing when it's your turn to talk. Think about it.

Jim, an engineer for a large construction company, says, "The last thing people want is to see you coming back to them saying, 'What were those things you wanted me to do?' I always bring a pen and notepad with me when I know it's likely I'll be asked to do things. Repeating your notes to the person is also a good idea—it lets you make sure you heard everything correctly, and it often reminds the other person of something he forgot to say."

Learn to Remember Names

Remembering someone's name can be hard to do, but if you can, the payoffs are tremendous. Don't you like it when people you have just met call you by name? You feel important in their eyes. When you call people by their name when talking with them, they are more likely to listen to you and respect you.

Listening is the first step in remembering a name. Be sure to listen intently when someone is introduced to you. Repeat the name immediately when you respond. "John, I'd like you to meet Sally McCormick from our Shipping Department." You say, "Nice to meet you, Sally," or, in case you need to clarify what you heard, say, "Sally McCormick? Nice to meet you." If you got her name wrong, this gives Sally a chance to correct you.

When you're new on the job, you'll have many new names to remember. People will understand for the first few weeks, so there's no harm in asking someone whose name you've forgotten: "I'm sorry, but I can't recall your name. Would you mind telling me again?" After the initial grace period, however, you may want to ask your coworkers to refresh your memory of others' names.

Some people use mental tricks to help them remember names. They associate a name with an object or an attribute that is easy to recall; for example, Joyce mentally calls Tom Allen, who is six feet, six inches, "Tall Tom." Just be careful not to let your mental name for a person slip out in conversation!

Control Your Reactions

You should also try to control how you respond to what is being said. If your boss is showing you how to prepare the monthly report and perhaps gets a little too basic, your first reaction may be to be insulted—he seems to think you don't know how to do the simple math involved. But in fact it could be that your boss remembers having problems in this area when he first did this report, and he's simply trying to help. Don't jump to conclusions without giving him the benefit of the doubt. The risk is that your brain will concentrate on the insult it thought it heard and drown out the rest of your boss's instructions. Then you'll really be in trouble.

The person speaking may use certain words that trigger an emotional response in you. Before you know it, you're thinking about the deeper meanings of those words instead of listening to the rest of what is being said. When this happens to you, recognize that words can have different meanings to different people. Try to concentrate on the context of what is being said, rather than on your interpretation of a few words.

Let's say your boss is giving you your first performance evaluation, and she says some things that you think are not true. Instead of jumping in and taking issue with her, stop and let her finish. Try your best to stay calm, even though you may be seething inside. Then tell her that you'd like the chance to correct the record or explain your side of the story. Ask her if you can get together later that day or the next to go over the problem. Try to avoid expressing your feelings right then and there—it's best if you can cool off a bit and have some time to absorb what she said and get your thoughts together. Tell her so at the end of your session.

When you think things over later, you may see that she had a point—you were just humiliated at the thought of failing at something. It may be something so small that you were more upset about it than she was. On the other hand, you may decide that she got things wrong, and you simply need to clarify the facts. Either way, when you meet again, you'll be in a more rational frame of mind and will be able to act professionally. Your boss will respect you for that and will be more likely to treat you with respect in the future.

No one likes to be criticized—it's not just you. And very few people are comfortable with or good at giving criticism, no matter how long they've been managers. That's because they know how much it can hurt, and they know they'll probably have to deal with an upset employee. If you can look at criticism, or "feedback," from your manager's point of view—that is, your boss is trying to help you learn your job and prepare you for your next one—then you may find it a little easier to take. Tell yourself it's your performance that's being commented on, not your worth as a person.

If you can take criticism well, you'll also be showing your boss that you are mature and concerned about correcting your mistakes. This is the attitude of a true professional.

Listen for the Meaning Behind the Words
In some situations it pays to try to figure out the true meaning of, or reasons behind, the words. Most managers dread giving

negative feedback of any kind, so they try to couch it in the gentlest terms possible. If you're not really listening, you could miss "hearing" something your boss would like to have corrected. For example, Ben's manager told him, "It's really important to let me know if you're going to be late to work." Here's what Ben's boss wanted to say: "You've been late too often lately, and you've compounded the problem by not letting me know about it. Your actions are irresponsible and unprofessional, and if they keep up, you'll be placed on probation." If you aren't sure you understand the full meaning of your boss's comments, then ask questions that will help you clarify it.

Avoid Interrupting

Try to avoid interrupting whenever possible. You probably interrupt occasionally to show that you're listening or to share your thoughts on the subject. If your boss is trying to explain something to you, however, it's best that you simply give your full attention and nod and say, "Yes, I see" or something similar from time to time. If you start to get lost, however, say so. Interrupting for this reason is perfectly acceptable.

Janet, an analyst with a small investment company, recalls, "When my boss would start to lose me on something, I must have gotten a totally confused expression on my face. He'd stop and say, 'It looks like I'm losing you—what don't you understand?' I learned that you should never pretend you understand or know something that you don't."

Pay Attention to Body Signals

If your boss calls you to her office, you can get a pretty good idea about the seriousness of the conversation by noting the way she sits at her desk—is she relaxed and smiling or stiff and expressionless? Of course, it might take awhile for you to get to know her well enough to figure out her moods and how she portrays them. Most experts agree, however, that if your boss fails to make eye contact with you, you're probably in trouble.

Watch your own nonverbal giveaways. Maintain frequent eye contact; if you look at the floor or out the window, your boss will think you don't care or aren't listening. Try not to play with your hair or drum your fingers on the table or tap your feet—these acts will reveal your nervousness.

Facial expressions are dead giveaways. Suppose your boss is giving you a new assignment, one you have decided is particularly distasteful. If you let this be known by frowning and perhaps sighing deeply, she will think you are a prima donna, not a team player. This is one of many occasions when you will want to suppress your true feelings for the good of your career.

Understand What You Hear

It's not easy to catch everything, especially during the first few months, when so much is new to you. Don't make the mistake of thinking that something you don't understand is not important, or that you'll figure it out later. If the speaker is going too fast for you, say so. If you don't understand a word or a term, ask for a definition. When the speaker finishes, say something like, "Okay, this is how I understand it—tell me if I'm off track," and then summarize what you've heard. If you're hesitant to do these things for fear of showing your ignorance, you'll only make matters worse later, when you'll make a mistake that will prove you didn't know something. The expression "There are no dumb questions" applies especially to people in their first jobs—most managers welcome questions and will not think less of you for asking. Bosses will, however, think less of people who don't ask and pretend to know it all.

Keep an Open Mind

It's human nature to hear what we want to hear or expect to hear. That's why paying close attention is so important—you could be surprised if you open up to hearing exactly what is being said.

There will be times when you have to listen to something you don't agree with or aren't especially interested in. Try your best to keep an open mind about it—you could learn something of value or see something in a different light. A closed mind never gets a chance to grow, yet growth is key to your success both on the job and off. If nothing else, you should learn to respect other viewpoints and ideas. No matter where you work or how long you work, you'll never find people you'll always agree with. If you realize this fact of life now, you'll avoid disillusionment and unnecessary conflict later.

Empathize

If someone who is normally upbeat and nice to you suddenly gets snappy or short, you'll tend to take it personally. Try not to. His attitude could be the result of a very bad day—his boss criticized him, he's coming down with the flu, or something is going wrong in his personal life. If it's a rare occurrence, brush it off rather than confront it and make matters worse for both of you.

Tolerate Difficult People

Some people will be, quite simply, a pain to listen to. They repeat stories, they complain, they talk about the same things day in and day out. It's hard to stay attentive and empathetic to people like this. If the person is a peer—that is, someone about your age and your level in the company—you can be a little more blunt about pointing out that you've heard the story once, and be more creative about avoiding the person. Otherwise, you'll have to exercise more restraint, if only for your own good. Always listen as considerately as you can, all the while looking for a believable means of escape. "Oh, there's Sandra! I've been looking for her all morning—got to run."

For true pests—say, the person who shows up at your desk on a regular basis to unload personal problems on you—you might try getting your neighbors to help out by calling you from a phone in another office, summoning you to an important but fictional meeting. This technique is pretty extreme but works well, and after a couple of times the person finds someone more responsive to latch on to.

MAKING YOUR BOSS HAPPY

When you start a job, one of the first things you should determine is the relative importance of the tasks you perform, so you'll know how to set priorities. Your boss will be able to tell you how to do this, but what she will not mention is that your real priority is to make her happy. This may sound self-serving, but it's a fact of business life. In the long run, if your boss is not happy with you, you're going nowhere, except perhaps out the door. The best way to keep your boss happy is simply to do a great job, but some other factors are crucial to maintaining a good working relationship.

Don't Cause Embarrassment

Sometimes it's the little things that count—like double-checking facts and figures, proofreading something twice, figuring out ways to make a report or presentation look better, answering the phone in a friendly, helpful manner. You may prepare work for your boss that her managers will see. Or you may work regularly with people in other divisions who view you as your division's primary contact. If you do anything that gets back to your boss and causes her embarrassment or gets her in trouble, she's not going to be too happy with you. On the other hand, if she gets praised for something that originated with you, she'll be both pleased and grateful.

If you find out that something's gone wrong, tell your boss *immediately.* She has a right to know about anything that affects her department, and you can be sure she'd rather hear it from you than from her boss or someone outside the department. If you don't tell her right away, two things will happen: She'll hear about it eventually and be embarrassed that she was the last to know, which suggests to others that she has an incompetent or disloyal staff. And you'll look as if you were trying to hide the problem. You'll be worse off than if you had told her in the first place. People have been fired for failing to keep their boss informed of problems.

> Justine, a staff member at a state college, recalls, "I was asked to deal with a situation in which one of our students was being racially harassed. I followed the protocol for handling such a situation and was able to resolve the problem quickly and effectively. But I made a big mistake—I forgot to tell my boss about it. When a story about the problem appeared in the school newspaper, I really got in trouble with her—she was embarrassed that she didn't know about the problem when *her* boss asked for details. All the good work I had done was overshadowed by my blunder."

Respect Your Boss's Time

Even though you shouldn't feel bad about asking lots of questions in your early weeks on the job, you should try to save them up instead of running to your boss with every question as it arises. You may even find an answer on your own or through someone else in the meantime. If you keep a running list and ask several questions at a time, you'll also demonstrate your organizational skills. The main point is to respect your boss's time—you're not the only person she must deal with during the day. When you're in her office to discuss something, be as brief and to the point as you can, unless it's obvious she's encouraging the conversation along.

If she invites you to meetings, be on time. If you're late, her colleagues and subordinates will think that she doesn't have the management skills to develop a responsible employee. The same applies for showing up for work on time and not taking frequent breaks and long lunches.

Work Hard, Work Smart

As obvious as this sounds, *working hard* means different things to different people. Some think that putting in the bare minimum amount of work is the same thing as working hard. Others have a low tolerance for any type of stress or deadline pressure and become martyrs if they have to skip a coffee break.

The only definition of hard work that counts is your boss's, and it may take you awhile to figure that out. If he's a workaholic and regularly spends ten-hour days at the office and then takes work home, you may look like a slacker if you put in your eight hours and leave. It depends—usually managers don't expect the same kind of output from their subordinates, especially at entry-level positions, unless the entire group is dealing with a heavy workload. But you can be sure your boss will not be pleased if you're out the door at the stroke of five on a day when everyone else is staying late.

Perhaps the best sign that you're working hard and smart is that you're able to finish projects and tasks on time. Always ask your boss how long he expects a task will take to complete. If you finish somewhere near that estimate, he'll know you're working hard. If it takes a little longer at first, don't worry—but if you're still bogged down by the third or fourth time you've done the same task, you may have a problem. Even then, keep in mind that managers tend to underestimate the time needed to do something, because they themselves may never have done it or did it so long ago they've forgotten. They may also be judging you against your predecessor. If she was a whiz, you may be in trouble, but if she was a little slow, you'll look good no matter what you do.

Working smart is the best way to get things done quickly and to reduce stress and boredom at the same time. Once you feel comfortable with a task, step back and take a look at ways you could do it more efficiently. Perhaps you could put a complex table into a spreadsheet program so that you could avoid doing a lot of math and extensive formatting. Even if you have to take time to learn the new program, it might be time well spent. Always check with your boss first, though, before making any major changes in the way you do things.

Knowing how to set priorities and then reorder them as events change is another part of working smart. In the beginning, you should check with your boss often to make sure the two of you have the same ideas about what is important and what isn't. Make a list and show it to her just to be sure. See Chapter 6, Getting the Job Done, for more on this topic.

Use your head. Try to understand your role in the office and how your work fits in with that of others. Think about the job you are doing, no matter how mundane or simple it seems. It's easy to fall into a mindless approach to tasks when work doesn't challenge us. But if you become robotic, you'll never have a chance to show others how much you have to offer.

Anticipate Your Boss's Needs

If you can think ahead to what your boss will need without him telling you, you will become his favorite person. You will probably have to be on the job awhile before you can do this, but it shouldn't be hard eventually to figure out the kinds of things he usually asks for. Perhaps he has asked once or twice in the past for you to make an extra copy of a certain report for a manager in another office. Don't wait to be asked the next time—make the copy and then mention, "I made a copy for Jim as well—is that correct?" Don't go overboard and presume too much, however. It's usually best to check first before doing something on your own. After awhile you'll get a better idea of how far you can go.

Communicate the Way Your Boss Does

Is your boss a "word" person? Does she like everything written up on paper so she can have a permanent record of events and conversations? Or is she devoted to her computer, especially the E-mail program, preferring on-line messages to memos? Whatever approach she takes, you should follow. She'll be that much more comfortable with you.

Be Dependable and Loyal

Always try to do what you say you're going to do; don't promise your boss you'll finish something by noon just to make him feel good, when you know it's unlikely you'll be through before five. Be dependable, not only by showing up on time but also by being consistent in the way you get things done. If your boss has to continually remind you to do certain things, you are not being dependable.

Loyalty to your boss and to the company means not tearing them down to others. It also means not divulging corporate information to those outside the company; even innocent remarks can hurt.

Honesty is of prime importance. See Chapter 5, Integrity at Work, for a discussion of what it means to be honest at work.

Be a Team Player

Probably the most disliked person in any office is the one who seems to be working toward personal goals, not those of the organization. You can spot this person fairly easily: He keeps to himself, he turns away offers of help even when deadlines are looming, and he takes all the credit for successes, even if others contributed. This kind of person, in turn, will not usually help you out, either. Sooner or later his uncooperative attitude catches up with him, and he is passed over for promotion to a higher-level job, where cooperation with other staff and managers becomes even more important for getting things done.

If you get pegged early on as someone who doesn't put the goals of your group or organization ahead of your personal agenda, people will begin to avoid you and perhaps even try to make life hard for you. If, on the other hand, you make the effort to find out what is important to group success and offer to help whenever you can (or whenever you are asked), you'll

quickly become an essential part of the team, and you'll probably find going to work much more satisfying. It's more fun when
you're an active player in a group effort.

What if you don't like some of your coworkers? Your first
instinct may be to avoid them, but resist that urge. The business
world is made up of all kinds of people and personalities, and
one of your goals in this first year should be to get over the idea
that you have to like people to work cooperatively with them.
Instead, try to look for the best in people, and if you can't do
that, at least learn to accept people as they are and to treat them
with respect. They probably won't change, and no amount of
complaining or wishful thinking will make much of a difference—except to make you more unhappy because you're
dwelling on it. See Chapter 4, Getting Along with Your Boss and
Your Coworkers, for more on this topic.

Learn What Your Boss Really Expects of You

This, unfortunately, is not as easy as it sounds. You'll have no
problem finding out how to do the basic parts of your job—
you'll be taught those things in your first few weeks. You may
even be given a formal job description that spells out in detail
responsibilities and expectations. And you may have a boss who
lets everyone know the goals of the group, whether general or
specific. But even if you think you know what's expected of you,
try to determine what the unspoken expectations are.

Some managers are always in a rush. They might routinely
assign a task to you, giving a few basic guidelines, and dash off
to a meeting. If you have any doubts about what you're supposed to be doing, ask. The best way when dealing with a busy
manager is to accumulate all your questions after you've had a
chance to think about the assignment and then put them in
writing, either on paper or in an E-mail message. By doing so,
you'll make it easy for your boss to answer each question, and
you can be sure you'll get all your questions answered.

Other managers are vague; sometimes you may wonder if

they've thought out the task they've given you. Again, don't be afraid to ask questions. Word them as specifically as you can, and word them so the answers you get will be helpful ones, not just more-ambiguous ones.

A frequent employee complaint is that managers make too many unrealistic assumptions. Your boss may think you already know something that you haven't had time to learn. He thinks you can get a ten-hour task done in five, or that you are aware of some unwritten company policy or practice. His problem is that he's forgotten what it's like to be new to the company. This is a sticky problem because you don't know what his assumptions are, and you can't ask questions about things you don't know. If you find yourself with this type of boss, you may have to remind him gently that you're new and unfamiliar with the corporate ways, although you're eager to learn. Open-ended questions like "Is there anything else I need to know about this before I start?" or "Who on the staff has done this before, so I can go to that person with minor questions?" can help. If you can find someone who has done the job in the past, you'll be able to get more details and clearer advice than you might from your boss.

Take Feedback and Criticism Gracefully

This is hard. Keep in mind that even the toughest-sounding people can be crushed by a critical remark. The secret is to view feedback as reflecting on your work only, not on you as a person—it's just a necessary part of learning the job. This distinction may seem like a fine line, but it's important to make. If you can find the courage to say, "Oh, I did that wrong" or "I came to the wrong conclusions" and then learn the right way and move on, you'll be a happier and more successful person in the long run. Some people are so afraid of being criticized or failing that they play it safe their entire career and never get anywhere. If you accept the fact that criticism is inevitable and an important part of professional growth, it will help you handle it better.

The worst bosses you can have are those who won't tell you if you've failed to meet their expectations. For example, Mark's manager was the type of person who hated to hurt anyone's feelings. When Mark made mistakes, she preferred to fix them herself or ignore them (if they weren't major ones) rather than tell him what he had done wrong. After a few months, these innocent mistakes led to more serious problems, and other departments started to complain to her. At this point, the boss had to talk with Mark. Unfortunately, she was somewhat angry and embarrassed, mostly at herself for failing to deal with the problem earlier. To make matters worse, the ensuing lecture was a complete shock to Mark; he thought he'd been doing a good job. He became frustrated and angry as well, because he felt his boss hadn't dealt fairly with him.

The best way to deal with this kind of boss is to ask frequently for feedback and then take any criticism of your work so calmly that your boss will eventually feel more comfortable about pointing out problems. If you can try to take feedback on a professional, not a personal, level, you'll be making a giant step toward your future success.

Susan began arriving at work later and later each morning, and offered no explanations. Her boss finally had to call her into his office and remind her of the importance of being on time. At first she was angry—she didn't think being on time was all that important as long as she got the job done—but her anger soon turned to tears. Her manager felt bad at first and tried to comfort her and play down the criticism. Later, however, he felt that her response was like a child's and knew he would be dreading to discuss with her any future problems that might arise. Holding back criticism may seem kind, but in fact it will hurt Susan in the long run because she won't be given the opportunity to learn from her mistakes.

All of this assumes that the person who is criticizing you is doing so fairly. If you feel that the comments are vague or even hostile, calmly ask for details and examples. If that fails, ask yourself what the person's motives might be, or what he or she may really be trying to say. If you see that the criticism is valid, go one step further and ask for advice on how you can do better next time. Even though this may be painful and certainly not much fun, you'll have demonstrated your maturity and willingness to learn. If you can take feedback and criticism gracefully, you will be seen as a confident, capable adult who has a strong sense of self-worth. It's an admirable quality to work on.

Show Initiative

Initiative in the business world means several things. It means keeping an eye open for tasks that need to be done and then doing them. It means thinking independently and creatively to look for better ways to get the job done. It means volunteering for extra work or special projects when your workload allows. It means managing your own work well so that your boss doesn't have to be reminding you of deadlines and duties. It means dealing with problems as they arise and not procrastinating or putting them aside in the hope they'll go away.

Takes initiative is a topic heading on just about every performance-appraisal form ever devised. Initiative is one of the most important traits you can have. Very few people have risen to top positions in their organizations without it. The amazing thing is that so few people show any initiative at all. They believe that as long as they're doing their job, they're doing well and will eventually be promoted. In fact, if they can't bring any added value to their work, they'll most likely be passed over for promotion. The days when time in a job automatically ensured a promotion are almost gone for good. To be promotable, you'll have to show your boss that you're able to handle the job. A boss who sees that you can think and act beyond the limits of your current job will feel a lot more comfortable in moving you ahead.

The good thing (for you) is that so few people do show initiative. Anything you do that's "above and beyond" will really stand out. Doing a little more than is expected of you is just not that hard, especially if you're not afraid to make mistakes every so often.

Bring Solutions, Not Problems

Most managers spend a good part of their day dealing with problems. If you have a question you can't solve on your own, you'll most likely bring it to your boss's attention. Now picture this: Your boss is embroiled in about eight or ten crises at the moment, and you bring in a relatively small problem. In fact, you have some ideas about a solution, but you just don't feel you have the experience or the authority to pick the right one on your own. If you can immediately proceed from stating the problem to offering some possible solutions, your boss will be forever grateful, as well as impressed at your ability to see solutions. You'll also demonstrate that your attitude is positive, even when you're dealing with a negative situation. And even if your boss has a better solution, you've still demonstrated that you can think on your own. Managers think highly of employees who can solve their own problems.

Understand Your Boss's Concerns

One manager puts it this way: If you really want to be valuable to your boss, try to figure out what keeps him up at night. In other words, if you can understand the kinds of things he worries about, you'll be in a better position to help him overcome those worries. You won't be able to do this right away, but after eight or twelve months on the job, it shouldn't be too hard if you've been paying attention.

HANDLING STRESS

Your first year on the job will have its stressful moments, you can be sure. How you deal with that stress will affect your performance, both now and later in your career. If you can learn the warning signs of stress and the best ways to manage it at this point, you'll be in a better position later on when you're at higher levels and must deal with even more stress.

Lynn recalls, "My boss told me a story about a fellow he once worked with who wasn't doing too well in the company. Around midnight one night he got a call from his boss, who asked him what he was doing. The man said, 'I was sleeping!' The boss replied, incredulously, 'How can you be sleeping while I'm up worrying about your future?' "

Stress can result from many things, and some people experience stress more readily than others. Here are some factors that can lead to stress at work:

- If you can never finish all you have to do in a day
- If the work is too difficult for you or doesn't make use of your strengths
- If the work atmosphere is harsh, threatening, or tense
- If certain people don't like you and give you a hard time
- If you feel torn in different directions, either between work and your personal life or between two factions at work
- If you feel thwarted by countless rules and regulations or a severe and demanding boss
- If you feel you're not doing a good job

You may not be aware of the stress you're experiencing—your brain can do a good job of repressing stressful thoughts, but your body will probably produce physical signs that reveal you're under stress. Here are a few examples:

- You have frequent headaches, stomach problems, skin problems, or neck or back pain.
- Your hair starts falling out.
- You feel nervous most of the time (do you fidget a lot or worry frequently about your job performance?).

- You can't seem to get a good night's sleep, and you feel tired all the time.
- You dream about workplace situations.
- You're overly irritable, and the smallest problems set you off.
- You start eating or drinking too much.

Chances are that you're expecting too much from yourself at this point in your career. If you have perfectionist tendencies, you'll be even more likely to feel stressed. Keep in mind that it's normal to feel stress whenever you're in a new situation. The key to keeping stress under control is to put things in perspective. Yes, it's important to get a report out on time, but you shouldn't feel like a total failure if you missed correcting a typo on page 2. You must tell yourself you did the best you could under the circumstances, then move on. If you dwell on mistakes and shortcomings, you'll just make matters worse, ruining your self-confidence and perhaps your health. Some people are harder on themselves than they would ever be on their subordinates; try to give yourself the same breaks you'd give someone else.

If you feel out of control—too much to do, too many conflicting priorities, too much that's new—stop and take a break for an hour. Draw up a to-do list, then put numbers by each item to indicate its priority. If you're not sure what should have priority, ask your boss to help. Sometimes just putting things on paper helps make them seem more manageable. If the items on your list have deadlines, write those down as well. If you have a lot of date-sensitive projects, you may want to transfer your list to a calendar so you can get a better picture of where you stand. See Chapter 6 for more techniques for getting your work under control.

Then tackle your desk and work area. If much of your job involves paperwork, put the related pieces of each task in a folder and label it. Then stack the folders in the order shown on your to-do list. You can then take each folder off the stack without thinking about what comes next.

At the end of the hour spent this way, you'll probably feel much more in control, and you may even realize that things are not as bad as they seemed. It's the *feeling* of being behind that magnifies our worries. If you can conquer that feeling, you will be able to better manage the stress.

If the cause of your stress seems to be other people, either at home or at work, try to talk with them to see if the problems can be identified and worked on. Again, you may find that you were assuming something that isn't the case. Perhaps you took a coworker's sharp comment as a personal affront, when in reality the person had been dealing with an irate customer and you just happened to walk in. If someone seems to be continually making things difficult for you, try to get up the courage to discuss the problem with that coworker head on. It probably won't make things worse, and you'll probably disarm the person so much that he or she will try to come around. The technique doesn't always work, but it's certainly worth a try.

Ashley, in her first job as a meeting planner, couldn't believe it when she learned that her predecessor kept track of all a meeting's myriad details with pencil and paper. "Even though I started the job during the busiest season of the year and had lots to learn as well, I decided to try to put everything into a computer program—those penciled notes just seemed so inefficient! But boy, did I regret it. I spent so much time trying to get everything to work on the computer that I had to work nights and weekends just to keep up. The stress was awful. I ended up having to use the paper system after all. Using the computer was a good idea, but I wish I had waited until I understood the process a little better and had more time to do such a big job right."

Finally, you may want to share your stress with your boss or your coworkers, but if you do, be cautious. There's a fine line between venting and complaining. If you're putting out a huge amount of work in a short time, a few complaints now and then are understandable. If you're not that busy and yet complain all the time, you'll look bad and annoy your boss and others. Everyone experiences stress from time to time, and you should consider that you're not the only one who feels pressured.

MAKING FRIENDS AT WORK

You'll find that you'll probably become personal friends with some of the people you work with, especially if your company is a large one. Many lifelong friendships, and even marriages, have begun in office settings. It may take awhile, even a year or two, before you get to know people well enough to form friendships, but in the meantime you should keep a couple of thoughts in mind.

First, pick your friends carefully. It will be hard to tell at first who the office troublemakers are, and you don't want to be too closely associated with them. How can you spot them? You can use your own good judgment for starters. Does the person seem to be well respected by others in the group? Does he or she exhibit professional behavior, or spend too much time chatting, passing on gossip, taking long lunches, or whining incessantly about how tough things are? Does the person try to get you involved in these kinds of activities? If you notice that the people you respect stay away from this person, you can be fairly sure you should, too. If you're still not sure, ask someone whom you trust what his or her opinions of the person are. Like it or not, you will be judged by the company you keep.

Second, avoid giving your friends special favors or treatment if you deal directly with them in your job. If you're the systems analyst and you stop everything to work on your friend's program, you'll be sure to make other people unhappy. They may even complain to your boss, and you don't want that to happen.

Third, try to make friends at all levels and departments in the company. You'll broaden your horizons and get to know the workings of your organization from several different viewpoints. You may even find that you'd love to work in another department someday and begin taking steps to do so. By having friends at different levels, you'll be viewed as someone who is interested in more than just your corner of the world, and this attitude can mean a lot when it comes time for promotions and transfers.

Participate in group lunches, office parties, and other social outlets that may be going on in your office. You don't have to go to them all, but if you don't attend your office mate's birthday lunch out, others will think you're unfriendly and antisocial.

Ellen remembers how a coworker of hers limited his promotion potential by keeping to himself: "At first Michael was invited to a number of social events after work, but he declined his coworkers' invitations. He even refused to go to the company picnic and holiday party. What he didn't realize was that these events were almost as important to his career as his work at the office. His manager would have liked to see how he conducted himself socially, and he missed out on getting to know people who might have helped him back at the office. His absence at these functions did nothing to help his career."

What about office romances? The standard advice is to try to avoid them, but the reality is that the office may be the only place you are going to meet people, especially if you're in a new city and haven't yet made friends outside the office. If it happens, do your very best to be discreet. Limit your "friendship" time with the other person at work, even to the point of not always having lunch together or stopping by his or her desk several times a day. People love to gossip about personal relationships, and your actions may affect how your boss and others perceive you.

For example, if the two of you are close in age and are at about the same level in the company, you may not have a problem. But it's still best to be low-key about it. If, on the other hand, your new love is an established manager there (heaven forbid it's your boss!), you could be getting into a dangerous situation. If you decide to do something drastic, like get married, one of you—probably you—may have to leave, depending on company rules about married people working together. You should also think about what might happen if the relationship breaks up. Will you be able to work with someone who has caused you pain in some way? Probably not, so be prepared to look for another job if you start an office romance.

If the person you're interested in is married, the best advice is to look elsewhere. Not much good ever comes from such a relationship, either personally or professionally.

If you're not interested in someone, but that person is obviously interested in you, be as blunt as you have to be. It's normal to want to be nice to people, but if you feel that someone is trying to get too close, make your wishes quite clear from the start. Otherwise, the person may not get the hint. One good way is to say you never date people you work with. (Of course, if he finds out you've been seeing Bob in Accounting, you have a problem. You also have to hope that the person doesn't leave the company in two months and then call you.) Be sure that you're not sending conflicting signals by flirting or making remarks about the sad state of your love life.

DEALING WITH CUSTOMERS

If your job puts you in contact with your company's clients or customers, your appearance, attitude, and skills will directly reflect on your employer. In fact, you *are* the company in your customers' eyes. If you speak or dress in a sloppy manner, your customers will form an opinion of your company as one that might give sloppy service or produce carelessly manufactured products. That's why your manager will care a great deal about how you come across to customers.

The two most important rules for dealing with customers are (1) be honest and straightforward at all times and (2) always do what you say you're going to do. If you return phone calls promptly, follow up on problems quickly and effectively, and treat the customer with respect, you'll do well. If you keep in mind the fact that the customer is responsible for your paycheck, it will help put things in perspective.

"The customer is always right." You've no doubt heard this phrase, but keep it in mind the first time you have to deal with an irrational, dissatisfied customer. The philosophy behind this saying is that a business cannot survive without its customers, and that making them happy is the single most important factor in a company's success. There's an old business adage that happy customers will tell two or three people about a good experience with a company, but angry customers will tell ten or fifteen people about a problem they've had. No company wants to risk that kind of bad publicity. According to another business axiom, if an unhappy customer can be made happy again, that customer will stay loyal to the company for life. It therefore is worth it to a company in the long run to keep people happy even if fixing the current problem costs time and money.

Carl notes, "In a small company, even one person who doesn't return phone calls quickly or follow up on jobs makes everybody else look bad by association. I feel that the client must think we're all irresponsible. We have someone like that where I work, and even though I shouldn't have to apologize for him, sometimes I feel I must."

Here are some things to keep in mind when dealing with an irate customer:

• Listen attentively and sympathetically to what the person is telling you. Try not to interrupt, but rather wait until the customer is finished to ask questions or to explain something.

• Keep your cool at all costs. This is not easy if the customer is on the warpath, but try very hard to remain calm and detached. Don't let the customer pull you into the fray.

• Don't make excuses. The customer doesn't care—and will probably resent—that the Shipping Department has been very busy with another customer's job. Also, try not to use the words "It's not our policy."

• Repeat back to the customer your understanding of the problem. Verify details like dates and times and amounts. Apologize for the inconvenience or trouble that has resulted.

• If you can easily solve the problem at this point, and you have the authority to do so, go ahead.

• If the problem or the customer's demands go beyond your ability to help out on the spot, explain that you must talk to your manager. Say this in a positive way, not in a way that suggests you're about to pass the buck. Stress that you will call the customer back by a certain (and reasonable) time with a resolution, and give her your full name and direct phone number so she can call if she has further questions.

• Make good on all your promises.

Keeping your word is the mark of a true professional. If your customers know they can count on you to (1) get back to them when you said you would, (2) keep them informed of any progress or delays, and (3) deal with them in a respectful, straightforward manner, you will be miles ahead of most of your colleagues. It's really not that hard, but surprisingly few people take the time or make the effort to treat others as they would like to be treated themselves.

Every so often you may have dealings with a customer who is truly abusive or tries to see how far you can be pushed. Be sure to keep notes about what was said and when; record every detail you can, because you or your boss might need it later to support your case. Tell your boss about the problem as soon as you realize you have one. If the customer isn't playing fair, you shouldn't have to put up with the situation.

Jeanne, a computer technician, tells what happened when she had to deal with an irate customer—one of her company's directors: "I was in her office trying to fix her PC when she blew up at me and demanded to know why my department couldn't get better equipment. I tried to explain to her that she needed to talk to my boss, that I couldn't really answer her questions. But she just kept yelling at me, and I took it because I knew I had to respect her position. When I left, she did say she knew it wasn't my fault, but she never really apologized. I always felt a little tension between us until the day I quit, almost a year after that incident. When she heard I was leaving, she gave me a hug and said, 'I feel really bad about that time I yelled at you. I'm really sorry.' "

AVOIDING PROBLEMS WITH DRUGS AND ALCOHOL

There's really only one thing to say on this subject. If your boss, or even anyone in your company, has reason to suspect you have a problem with drugs or alcohol, your reputation and your future in the job will be at risk. The general feeling is that such people cannot be trusted to act professionally at all times, and that keeping them is never worth the cost in lost customers, contracts, or company reputation.

KEEPING YOUR PRIVATE LIFE TO YOURSELF

If you're having personal problems of any kind—emotional, financial, or physical—it's best to keep them to yourself. Share them with your boss if you think they may affect your work, but give as little detail as possible and assure your manager you have things under control. Don't share your problems with anyone unless you want the entire office to know. Even your closest friends may accidentally pass along confidential information.

Even if you don't mind people knowing about your problems, divulging them could have an effect on how people treat you. For example, you may miss out on being assigned to the year's most visible project because the manager feels that you can't be counted on to be fully dedicated. You may inspire sympathy, but you won't be considered reliable.

It's easy to let a personal problem consume your time at work. Try to limit absences, lateness, personal phone calls from your desk, and so on. People will notice and assume your mind is not on your work. Don't risk adding job performance problems to your life at this point. Many people who have been through tough personal times say that concentrating on their work was helpful, because it let them focus their energies on more positive and productive challenges.

If you have a problem that is beyond your ability to solve on your own, don't hesitate to get help. Many companies provide employee assistance programs (EAPs), usually staffed by psychologists and social workers, that are highly confidential. The company contracts with an outside organization to provide short-term counseling and referral services in all aspects of business and personal life, including problems relating to finances, marriage, children, parents, and work. This service is usually provided free or at a very low cost to the employee. Check your employee manual or call your Human Resources office for more information. One warning: If your boss strongly recommends that you seek assistance through the EAP, be sure to do so. If your problem is affecting your work to the point that your manager brings up this program, you may be in danger of losing your job. If you refuse to take advantage of such a program, management may use your refusal as grounds for dismissal. The EAP will not divulge anything about the discussions you have with the program, but it can let your company know if you received help there.

COPING WITH OFFICE POLITICS

What is meant by *office politics*? In its most basic sense, the term refers to the way people interact with each other to achieve personal and group goals. It has to do with gaining power, which in corporate life also means gaining money and prestige. Most of us would like to think we can avoid getting involved in such distasteful-sounding business, but the reality is that everyone is affected by it and everyone "plays politics" one way or another.

When you offer to help out a colleague who is struggling to meet a deadline, your intentions may be good, but deep down you're probably thinking, "Now maybe Scott will help me if I'm ever in a pinch." Doing and returning favors is one aspect of office politics.

When a person or a group tries to gain favor or control, things can get a little messier. Groups may be pitted against one another in a competitive way, which management may encourage because it thinks "contests" are a good way to get the most out of people. But often the backbiting and bad feelings that result diminish the company as a whole and make it hard for the employees to focus on shared goals. It may be tough at first for you to understand why there is such tension in the office. If you realize that rivalry among some employees is the cause, you may see why some people act the way they do.

Lying, for example. Cathy, who works in your department, is on a fairly obvious campaign to make herself look good to your boss. She sees you as the biggest threat to her advancement and has decided to make you look bad to the boss whenever she can—carefully, of course. She may give you the wrong time or date for an important meeting, or intercept a phone call intended for you. Or she will criticize your work to others behind your back, so that they will go to her, not you, for help with their projects. There aren't too many people like this around, but you should know they exist and watch out for them.

On the positive side, you can enhance your own career by

practicing some of the good aspects of office politics. If you are easy to work with, are willing to help out, and can develop a reputation for honesty and efficiency, people will want to have you on their team. In fact, if you have these characteristics, people will seek you out. And the more people in the company who know you, like you, and can count on you, the better off you'll be when you're ready to move around or move ahead. The process is known as getting "visibility" to those higher up on the corporate ladder.

SUMMARY

To put it in a nutshell, someone who is a true business professional—

- Maintains a positive, friendly attitude
- Refrains from whining and complaining
- Knows that it's better to say too little than too much
- Refrains from bad language and off-color jokes
- Knows how to listen for content and meaning, not merely to the words
- Knows that making the boss happy means seeing the world from his or her point of view
- Keeps personal problems out of the office
- Readily admits mistakes and learns from them
- Doesn't make excuses
- Is open to new ideas and experiences
- Is leery of romantic entanglements in the workplace
- Treats customers with care and respect
- Is a team player
- Can be trusted
- Does what needs to be done without being told
- Knows what's expected of him or her
- Takes criticism gracefully

Getting Along with Your Boss and Your Coworkers

This job would be great if it weren't for the people."

Many a frustrated employee has made this statement at one time or another. The irony, of course, is that it's hard to think of a job where you wouldn't have to work with people. Even if you love your work and get along fine with almost everyone, you'll be miserable if you let even one difficult person get the best of you.

Notice the word *let* in the previous sentence. It's there for a reason: Always remember that even though you can't control what another person says or does to you, you can control your reaction to it. This mind-set is tough to put into practice, but if you can, you'll be a happier person in the long run.

Another key to success in working relationships is to accept people for who they are. Nobody is perfect, and certainly nobody, not even you, will ever measure up to your definition of perfect. People will disappoint you, make you angry, make you cry, make you feel low. Sometimes they mean to, but most of the time they do not—it's simply the way they are. You'll encounter an amazing variety of people in your working career, each unique and with good points and bad. You can't change them, so don't even try. At times you'll have to let things roll off your back—so you can get on with your job. Sometimes forgetting (and even forgiving) is the best thing you can do.

Many times you'll have to restrain yourself from saying what's really on your mind. Is this being dishonest? No, it's staying in control and staying professional. It means you're keeping the greater goals in mind.

In her book, *Dearest Amanda . . .: An Executive's Advice to Her Daughter,* Eliza Collins sums it up well:

> Success comes from being able to handle the intimate and complex human relationships that make up a workplace community. After a certain point, your functional skills will count less and less. What will matter is how you treat other people, how other people see you, how you handle the disappointments that are inevitable, how you balance the conflicts that arise. . . .

GETTING ALONG WITH YOUR BOSS

You may think that the most important part of your job is to perform the tasks outlined in your job description. But the really important part is to keep your boss happy. If you think about it that way, you'll see that you don't need to admire or like your boss, just get along with him or her reasonably well. You'll eventually have a boss you simply can't tolerate. When this happens, there are basically three things you can do:

1. You can complain loudly, suffer in silence, or alternate between the two.
2. You can quit.
3. You can learn to deal with the situation, at least for a while.

If you complain about your boss to other people in your office, you may get some sympathy for a while, but more likely you will become known as a chronic whiner, which goes against the professional image you need to cultivate. You also take the chance that your comments will make their way back to your boss. If you suffer in silence, you may *seem* to be handling things more professionally, but eventually your frustrations will make you truly miserable, and you'll want to quit, regardless of the consequences.

Daniel, a graphic artist, says, "I've found that not venting the stress that results from 'suffering in silence' can end up releasing itself in the form of a confrontation at work. Later, of course, you wish it had never happened."

If you quit your job to get away from one problem, you may find you have a few new ones—being unemployed, for example, or having a résumé that suggests a tendency toward job-hopping. When prospective employers ask you why you left your last job, be careful not to say it was because you couldn't get along with your boss—this would surely be a concern to any future boss. And even if you find a new job right away—or had one lined up before you quit—you may find out after a few months that your new boss is worse than your old one.

The best option is usually to learn to cope with your boss, at least for a while. "A while" might be several months or even two or three years, if you like everything else about your job. If nothing else, you'll get experience in dealing with difficult people, something that will always come in handy. Try looking at your first year on the job as a form of graduate school education in the field of human behavior, and turn a bad situation into one you can learn from.

The exception to sticking it out for a while is if your boss is clearly harassing you or asking you to do something morally or legally wrong. We'll talk more about that problem in Chapter 5, Integrity at Work. So how can you take control of what seems to be a bad situation? It may be hard to face, but start by making sure that your own assumptions or actions are not causing the problem.

Ron, a loan officer for a mortgage company, had a boss who was widely viewed as "difficult." She constantly criticized and corrected Ron's work, and Ron felt he could do nothing right. He finally found another job and soon realized that as a result of his experiences with his difficult boss, his work habits had changed: He had learned to be much more careful and pay close attention to detail, characteristics that greatly pleased his new boss.

Your Boss Is Not Your Mother

If you think about it, your first real job is probably the first time you are being treated like an independent adult. In college, you may have felt as if you were treated as a grown-up, but in fact your professors were supporting you in your transition to the real world. It may not have always seemed like it, but they were there to help you along. Your parents may respect you as an adult, but they'll still worry about you and continue to see you as their child, no matter how old you are. Your boss, on the other hand, sees you as an adult and will expect the same responses from you as from an older employee.

Don't go into your first job expecting to hear your boss's constant approval. You may be used to getting praise and encouraging words from your professors and your parents, but it's unlikely that you'll get much positive feedback from your boss. She may think you're terrific, but it's a fact of work life that very few managers feel the need to give compliments except for extraordinary efforts. So don't get discouraged if your boss says little about your performance—it doesn't necessarily mean you're doing a bad job or your boss is unappreciative.

If your boss does criticize some aspect of your performance, try to put those comments in perspective. Don't take them as a personal affront or a judgment on your worth as a human being. Separate your *self* from the tasks and skills that are part of your job. If your boss tells you that your math is wrong for the third month in a row on your monthly report, don't feel that you are pitifully incompetent and not worthy of even the simplest job—instead, just vow to yourself that you'll double-check and even triple-check your numbers next time.

Also, don't expect that your boss will be your mentor. Some managers are not interested in mentoring, for several reasons: They may see you as a threat, they don't enjoy teaching, they don't care about your advancement, or they simply don't have the time. Others just don't have the inclination. If you want a mentor, perhaps a coworker or other manager will take an interest in your growth. If you can find someone who has been very successful and has a solid knowledge of the field, you're lucky—a mentor can be a valuable ally and teacher of real-world lessons.

Not all career counselors believe that mentors are necessary. Some feel that you can avoid the disadvantages of a mentoring relationship by simply looking to successful people whose traits you admire and then following their example. Others believe that you should look outside your company for someone in your industry who can give you guidance that is more objective and comes from a broader perspective. One disadvantage of having a mentor in your own company is that you may become too closely identified with that person. This situation may become a problem for you if he or she falls out of favor with upper management.

Your Boss Has Problems, Too

It's always hard to know the problems that other people in your office are facing, whether the problems are personal or job-related. It's usually safe to assume that everyone has a share of both at different times. Try to keep this thought in mind when people, especially your boss, act in ways you don't understand.

Your boss may have several other people reporting to him, and any one of them could be causing him problems at a given time. If he isn't paying much attention to you, but spending a lot of time with your coworker down the hall, you can assume he's trying to deal with some sort of problem. One management rule of thumb is that 20 percent of the people take up 80 percent of a manager's time. If this is the case, be glad it's not you, and try to understand if your boss seems to be ignoring you.

> Judy, a sales associate, recalls, "We sort of liked it when our boss ignored us—it meant we weren't in trouble. We figured that no news was good news."

Your boss may be under pressure from her manager for any number of reasons. If you ever get a surprise mandate to fix something or change the way you do things, it could be that the order came from *her* boss, even though she may not tell you so. In short, there could be—and probably is—much going on in your company that you know nothing about. If you did, it might explain a lot. But you probably won't know, so the best approach is to accept the fact that people's motives and actions may have sources you're not aware of.

Your boss may also be experiencing personal problems that you may or may not know about. If his marriage is faltering, if his kids are acting up, or if his health is worrisome, cut him a little slack. He will have bad days where he might snap at you for some minor infraction, and days when he simply won't be himself. Some employees are so sensitive to their boss's moods and actions that they take any slights or harsh words personally. If your boss says or does something that just doesn't seem in character, consider that other things may be going on in his life. If your boss is in a bad mood all the time, then that's another matter. Either way, you're probably not the reason.

Are You Meeting Your Boss's Basic Requirements?

Any boss will be unhappy if an employee fails to exhibit certain basic behaviors and traits. These are rarely discussed but almost universally expected. Here they are:

- Competence
- Productivity
- Obedience
- Respect
- Trustworthiness
- Loyalty

Competence is the ability to do what you were hired to do. If you reveal after a few months on the job as an editorial assistant that you can't spell and never really understood the rules of grammar, your boss will be disappointed. She may even be angry at herself for making such a poor hiring decision. If you've been there six months and still ask for help with the most basic aspects of your job, you will also have an unhappy boss. Remember the 80–20 rule of thumb mentioned a few paragraphs earlier? If your boss is spending a lot of time with you trying to repair mistakes you made, you can assume that *you're* the problem, not your boss.

If you do the job you were hired to do, and then do just a little more than expected, you will stand out. One interesting fact of business life is that it takes surprisingly little extra effort to surpass expectations, regardless of where you are on the corporate ladder. Once you're known as someone who does a terrific job, you'll have a different problem: Your boss won't want to let you go!

Productivity means that you will accomplish the expected amount of quality work in the expected amount of time, and then some. If no one tells you what's expected, it's up to you to find out. Don't wait until you're off on vacation and the person who fills in for you tells your boss that she could do your job in half the time. Productivity also means that you can communicate quickly and clearly. You don't waste your time or the time of others. You look for ways to be efficient. You check your work carefully before turning it in, so that it doesn't have to be redone later.

Obedience is the habit of cheerfully—or at least without frowns, groans, or complaints—carrying out whatever your boss asks you to do, in the time frame expected. Managers use the term *insubordination* when referring to employees who blatantly ignore or disobey requests or instructions. Insubordination is a firing offense in most companies. A boss who asks you to do something expects that you will simply do it, not argue about it or later decide you'd rather not. This is one of the harsh realities of the business world that may come as a shock if you've lived a fairly democratic, unauthoritarian existence up to this point. Never forget that most businesses, deep down, are of necessity authoritarian; people are paid to carry out its necessary tasks. If you don't wish to do the task, you are free to leave the company.

This is not to say that you must remain silent about something you strongly disagree with. Let your boss know your feelings as diplomatically as you can, but also make it clear that you will do the task in the meantime. If you follow this suggestion, you are behaving in a professional way while holding to your own beliefs.

Respect means that you will recognize your boss's position and authority and treat her accordingly. This covers everything from observing common courtesies to appreciating the many demands on her time. If your boss comes to your desk to talk, stop what you're doing and give her your full attention. If you disagree with something she says, control your desire to argue with her or to correct her way of thinking. You should let her speak without a lot of interruptions. If you go to her office to ask some questions or to report on your progress, you should stand until you're offered a seat. You should be brief, to the point, and prepared; if you aren't, she'll begin to dread your visits as a waste of time.

Being *trustworthy* means that you'll always be honest and up front with your boss and coworkers. You can be relied on. You'll do what you say you're going to do, and you won't try to mislead or misinform anyone. You follow company policies and avoid any conflicts of interest. You'll protect confidential and proprietary information. You're honest, won't betray a confidence, and perform to the best of your abilities. People can count on you to follow through on tasks and to show up when expected. You can get the job done well, and on time. And if you don't know how to do something, you say so rather than fake it.

Lynn relates this story about respect for your boss: "Four of us, including our boss, were working with our client on a computer installation. At one point our boss asked one of us for a disk he already had in hand. My coworker, in the most sarcastic tone you can imagine, said to our boss, 'Are you blind? It's right there!' I couldn't believe my ears. I guess he thought he could get away with it because all of us, including our boss, are about the same age—in our twenties. But what got me was that he would treat our boss that way in front of our client. Our boss talked to him about it later. It seems the problem was that my coworker had never worked in a formal corporate environment before and didn't realize how unprofessional he had been—although his remark would be considered rude in any case."

Loyalty means that you will not complain about, criticize, berate, or otherwise paint a negative picture of your boss or the company to others, either inside or outside the company. It also means that you will do whatever you can to make your boss and your company look good and succeed.

If you fail your boss in any of these areas, he or she won't be happy with you. If you meet these basic needs and also do the following, your boss will feel lucky to have you:

- Keep your boss informed of problems and progress.
- Solve problems before your boss has to get involved.
- Tell your boss good news and bad, as soon as it happens.

- Make sure any ideas you propose are well thought out and workable.
- Volunteer for undesirable assignments.
- Save the company time and money.
- Help the company make money.
- Don't complain unless you have possible solutions.
- Accept criticism and learn from it.

> Sometimes being honest and trustworthy can make up for lesser flaws, as Danielle explains: "A guy in my office is constantly late and a little on the arrogant side. Our boss told me that although those problems are a concern to her, on the whole she respects him because she knows that he'll never lie or intentionally do anything to hurt anyone."

Many of these traits and behaviors are discussed elsewhere in this book. They're included here as a reminder that your actions affect how your boss treats you. That said, there are bosses who can make your life miserable, regardless of the kind of employee you are.

THE FIVE BASIC TYPES OF BAD BOSSES

Most managers don't take joy in being difficult; in fact, most are trying to do a good job. As one wise person put it, "Never attribute to malice what can be explained by incompetence." To be a really good manager requires a certain combination of skills, knowledge, and personality that is not easy to come by.

Many people become managers because they've been around a long time and it's the next step on the promotion ladder, not because they relish the idea or even think they'll be good at it. Others would rather be the boss than be bossed. Most people go into managerial positions because they think they'll be able to do a better job than their predecessor; later they find out how difficult it can be. Instead of having to please one boss, a manager must learn how to please two groups—upper management and employees. The boss is always in the middle.

In your case, there's also a good chance that your manager may be in her first supervisory job, and she may not be much older than you. If that's the situation, you're learning how to be a good employee at the same time your boss is learning how to be a manager. Mistakes and misunderstandings are bound to happen.

Once you've ruled out the possibility that your actions (or lack thereof) are the cause of any troubles you have with your boss, consider that he or she might fall into one of the five basic types of bad bosses most of us encounter at some point in our careers: the control freak, the power seeker, the spineless wonder, the distant boss, and the silent boss.

The Control Freak

Also known as a micromanager, this boss will spend a good deal of time with you during your first days and weeks making sure you understand every aspect of your job. The problem is that even when you're ready to go solo, she's still looking over your shoulder, seemingly waiting for you to slip up. If you write a memo or report, she rewrites it. If you decide to do certain tasks in a different order, she wants a full justification. She may even make critical or sarcastic remarks about your intelligence or abilities. These kinds of actions are particularly likely if your boss once held the job you have now. She may feel diminished or threatened if someone can do it as well as she did.

This type of boss is basically a control freak. Her motives are pure, though—she feels completely responsible for everything that goes on in her department and has a hard time believing that things will be done correctly. In fact, she's probably been burned in the past by employees who dropped the ball or made mistakes that got her in trouble with her manager. She's probably insecure and lives in fear that her reputation could be destroyed at any time by the people who work for her. If she's a relatively new supervisor, she may be having a hard time learning how to manage the work versus doing it. Some people are happier when their work is hands-on; they never do become good managers.

The best way to deal with this type of boss is to do the most careful job you can and to keep her informed of your progress. If she has to ask you about the status of something, take this as a hint that you're not keeping her sufficiently informed. Ask her how often she wants progress reports. Listen carefully to everything she says (taking notes to be certain), and don't be afraid to ask questions to make sure you understand what she expects of you. If she asks you to let her know when you've completed a particular task, be sure to do so. Just drop by her office or send her an E-mail that says you've finished it. After a while she'll feel comfortable with you and won't hover so much.

It's easy to feel intimidated and downtrodden if you have a boss like this. If things don't improve, you may feel you have to move on. In the meantime, try to understand your boss's motives and don't take things too personally. Her manager may be aware of the problem, and unbeknownst to you is getting ready to move your boss to a nonsupervisory position. If you like everything else about your job, it may pay to lie low and simply do a good job for a year or two. If your boss moves on, you could be in a good position to take over.

Also keep in mind that many managers just don't realize how intimidating they can appear to those who work for them. What your boss thinks is a straightforward request may sound like a brutal order to your ears. Consider these typical phrases:

- You need to . . .
- I need you to do . . .
- I have to have this as soon as possible . . .
- This is a priority . . .

Even if you cringe at hearing your boss make requests that begin with these words, keep in mind that she probably doesn't mean to sound so dictatorial. On the positive side, your experience will make you a more sensitive manager down the road, since you'll remember how these phrases sounded to you.

Employees often give great weight to the most insignificant actions a boss takes (just because your boss asked you to redo your monthly report doesn't mean you're about to be fired). Before taking harsh-sounding words too personally, try putting yourself in your boss's place. How would you be speaking to your employee?

Pam remembers an incident with her first boss: "One morning, Jerry dropped a report on my desk and told me to redo it. Then he stormed away. I looked over the report and couldn't figure out what I'd done wrong. I waited about ten minutes and then went to his office. In a soft tone I asked him to tell me exactly what he wanted me to change. By my tone of voice, he realized that he had been too abrupt with me. He actually apologized for being rude and took the time to explain what he wanted. I learned that you should never respond to anyone in a rude way, even if they've been rude to you."

It may not seem like it at the time, but the control freak is the best of the bad types of bosses to have. If nothing else, you'll get plenty of feedback and lots of experience in dealing with this type of person. There are quite a few of them around, and your first such boss probably won't be your last.

The Power Seeker

This boss is completely self-centered. You are important to him only in how you help him meet his goal of getting ahead and looking good to his superiors. For some reason he thinks that the normal rules of business and morality don't apply to him— but they do apply to everyone else, including you. He has no solid core of values, just the need to look good. He may drive a high-status car and wear expensive clothes. Deep down he may be insecure and not too sure of his worth. His external show of power and wealth helps him mask his insecurities.

It's fairly easy to keep this kind of boss happy. As long as you can make him look good and feel good (flattery will get you everywhere), he'll be happy. Remember that appearances are all-important. He also wants your admiration and respect, much more so than a normal boss. Just be especially tactful if you must tell him something negative.

If he makes promises to you—about special assignments, raises, promotions—try to see that they're put in writing, even if you have to send him a memo stating your understanding of what he said. He may not like your doing this, but do it anyway. He could change his mind tomorrow, depending on which way the wind is blowing. Don't get caught out in the cold.

The Spineless Wonder

This type of boss seems great at first—he leaves you alone, doesn't make too many demands, and is happy for you to do all of your work and perhaps a little of his. But after a while you begin to realize that he's not much help if you get in a bind or find yourself unable to carry out a complex assignment. "You can handle it. I know you can," he'll say. And then he'll disappear until you fail, when he will reappear to criticize your work (because now you've made him look bad to his boss).

This kind of manager is afraid to make decisions and hates confrontations of any kind. He's eager to please, and fearful to displease, upper management. He may not stand up for you or your group. You may find yourselves taking on extra assignments and putting in long hours because *his* boss knows he won't say no. You may find that he tells you something one day and the virtual opposite a month later. He's not doing this to make you crazy. He just doesn't remember what he said—or someone has come up with another idea and your boss goes along with that plan. In its worst form, this means that he's unreliable and perhaps not to be trusted, and you'd be wise to get things in writing, such as promises of raises, promotions, or plum assignments. As with the power seeker boss, the best way to do this is to draw up a quick memo stating your understanding of his expectations, along with the timetables you talked about, and send him a copy that tactfully asks him to verify your impressions.

This type of boss will be quite vague when assigning tasks and projects. He may simply be passing down work that his manager has given to him, and in fact he's not really sure how to do it himself. But, he figures, that's why he has you—he loves to delegate. To deal with this situation, ask your boss as many specific questions as you can. Try to pin him down, even if he has to admit he'll have to find out and get back to you. Again, it may be a good idea to state your understanding of an assignment in writing and ask for his approval. If you make the mistake of going ahead without a clear idea of what's expected of you, you could get burned later. Then it will be *you* that looks bad, not he.

This person may have been promoted because of his technical skills, not his managerial skills, which means he may tend to rely on you and others to handle sensitive coworker or client relationships. You may not mind this, but be careful. You might be putting yourself in difficult situations that could be over your head, and you may catch the blame if things go wrong.

The spineless wonder is in over his head. At times you have to feel sorry for someone who lives in such fear of revealing his incompetency. This person has usually developed good social skills, however, and is often well liked, which is one reason he's gotten as far as he has. He will want you to like him, even to be his friend. Here again, your goal is to outlast him or to move elsewhere in the organization. If you do good work and get along well with other managers, your chances of moving up are probably good.

The Distant Boss

If you work in a large group that reports to a single manager, you may have little interaction with that person. So many middle management jobs have been eliminated in the past few years that it's not unusual for managers to have twenty or more employees reporting directly to them. You may rarely work with or even see this kind of boss because she's just so terribly busy. The bad news for you is that you'll get little guidance and encouragement in your first job, something you really should hope for.

To avoid feeling like a cog in a wheel, you can do a couple of things. First, try to find a fellow employee to whom you can go for help and advice. In large groups there's often someone who looks out for new employees, even without getting the pay and recognition for it. Be sure the person you latch on to doesn't mind your questions and has been there long enough to give you good answers.

Second, try to get your boss's attention from time to time. But whatever you do, don't just drop by her office to chat. Have something of value to discuss—an idea, a problem she can help with, an achievement you're proud of. Call or send an E-mail to ask to set up a time that's good for her. Tell her you'll promise to keep it to ten or fifteen minutes—and then live up to that promise if she agrees to see you. Be very well prepared so that you can get right to the point. Try to muster all the confidence you can before going in—you'll gain more respect if you're not overly apologetic or shy. Try to keep such meetings to a bare minimum; you don't want to become a pest, and you don't want to look like an apple-polisher to your coworkers.

The Silent Boss

The boss who never criticizes, never corrects, never steps in is probably the worst type of boss you could have. Why? Because you won't learn anything, and when you move on to your next job, you could be in for a rude awakening. The silent boss is so nice that she wouldn't think of hurting your feelings by correcting something you did.

The other problem with this kind of boss is that she may shut you out if you do something that displeases her. But you'll never know what you did "wrong," because she doesn't have the nerve to confront you. If your performance continues to lag, she will tell her manager that you've become a problem, and the next thing you know you've been transferred or fired. This type of boss is also notorious for coming up with unpleasant surprises at performance appraisals, because she feels obliged (and perhaps allowed) to bring up unpleasant subjects at that time. Be aware that it is considered unfair and very poor management practice to bring up problems for the first time at the performance appraisal. You have a right to complain if that happens.

This kind of boss just isn't doing her job as a manager. You can try to encourage her to give you feedback, both positive and negative, by directly asking her how she thought you handled a project or wrote a report. In other words, if you bring up the subject of your performance or your problems, she may feel more comfortable discussing such things with you. Try hard to take any negative comments well and without argument, or else she'll be hesitant to open up the next time you ask.

As with the distant boss described earlier, you may have to befriend someone in your group who is willing to serve as your surrogate boss, who can help you learn the ropes and solve problems. If you can arrange this type of mentoring, you'll be better prepared for your second job.

Two Bosses Are Not Better Than One

In some offices, the lines of authority are not well defined. You may be told to go to your boss's boss when your boss is not available. Or your boss's boss may go around your boss and come straight to you with requests and assignments. It may be that your job requires you to report to two managers, or you may be loaned to another department for a few hours or days a week.

The basic problem is that you have two bosses, whose requests often overlap or conflict. You may have no choice but to do what you're told, but there are a few techniques you can use to stay out of trouble.

Maria's boss, Joan, told her to go to the director of their division whenever Joan was out of town, which was often. Maria found that every time she asked the director for guidance, he would give her a couple of new assignments to complete or change some aspect of a current assignment. The problem was that Joan was usually unaware of these additional tasks, and Maria wasn't sure how to reprioritize her work. Sometimes her workload got too much for her, but she didn't want to complain to the director and often had to wait several days before she could talk with Joan.

Maria's managers have placed her in an unfair position. The only way for Maria to keep her sanity is to shift the responsibility for determining priorities back to one of her managers. For example, on Monday Joan gave Maria a week's worth of work and left town, and on Tuesday the director added a daylong task to the mix. Maria should immediately tell the director about the tasks Joan gave her and ask him to help her decide which ones should be done first. Her question may be enough to make the director wait until he discusses things with Joan. Or if he does set priorities, at least Maria can later explain to Joan that she followed the director's instructions.

It's perfectly reasonable to feel that you must obey the most senior person around. Unfortunately, this is also unfair to your immediate manager, who may feel undermined and unimportant. Whenever you can, let your boss know right away about any tasks someone else has asked you to do, especially if doing them will jeopardize the work you're doing for your boss. She has a right to know, and if she can't—for whatever reason—change the situation, she may be able to get you additional help or reassign some of your work. Note that this advice does not apply to simple five- or ten-minute tasks from other managers that are a normal part of your job.

To Sum Up . . .

If you have a bad boss, one of the best ways to cope is to set some personal goals and work toward reaching them. Perhaps you can decide to learn a new software program in the months ahead. Try setting personal productivity goals, such as seeing how much you can accomplish by five o'clock or turning in work with no errors. No matter what your boss says (or doesn't say), you'll have the satisfaction of accomplishing something of value to you. And your efforts will give you something of value to discuss in future job interviews.

The added benefit of doing a good job, other than your own personal reward, is that others are bound to notice. Nevertheless, you may need to do some subtle self-promotion from time to time just to make sure they are aware of your accomplishments. This tactic may prove to be your best way out of a bad situation in the long run. Keep your eyes on openings and expansions in groups where you'd like to work, and make it known (discreetly if possible) that you'd be interested in joining them. Apply for any posted job openings you're interested in; don't assume that others know you'd like to leave your current position. (Do let your boss know you've done this, however.)

No matter what, always treat your boss with respect, whether or not you think he deserves it. Any positive achievements you've made will vanish in the eyes of your colleagues if you are rude, arrogant, or discourteous to your boss. People will notice and comment on your lack of respect rather than empathize with your plight.

There may be times when talking to your boss's boss about a problem is appropriate. A lot depends on how well you know that person and how long you've been unhappy—make sure it's at least six to twelve months. The first thing your boss's boss is going to ask you is, "Have you talked about this problem with your manager?" If you haven't, don't be surprised if he tells you to try to work it out before getting him involved.

If you have made your boss aware of your concerns yet no

changes have occurred, then you have a stronger case to present to his boss. Make sure you have gathered all the facts and can present them clearly and briefly. Whatever you do, don't launch into a personal attack on your boss; keep your statements factual and objective.

Going around your boss, even if the company says it supports an open-door policy, can be tricky. You might be seen as a troublemaker if the two bosses are staunch allies or personal friends. Try to figure out their working relationship before doing something that could backfire on you.

The truly difficult problems occur on the personal level. One scenario in particular is worth mentioning. Your boss seems to take little interest in you professionally but a lot of interest in you personally. He or she may ask a lot of questions about your personal life—more than those normally expected in a business relationship. Inappropriate jokes, comments, or perhaps a sexual advance may follow. At this point, and ideally earlier, you must make it clear that you are not interested and in fact are offended. It may be hard for you to be firm or discourteous to someone who has a good position in the company and seems to be well respected. Nevertheless, you must emphasize the seriousnesss of your request that such inappropriate behavior stop. If you try to make light of it in a pleasant way, the person may simply think you're playing along and continue to bother you.

If your clear requests to cease and desist are ignored, you should report the problem to Human Resources. This advice goes for *any* form of harassment that persists after your initial objections, including remarks and actions that reflect discrimination based on race, sex, physical disability, or religion. If you're not sure whom to talk to, ask the HR person you dealt with when you joined the company. Be sure to have a written record that describes the incidents and the dates they occurred.

Here's a completely different problem: What if your boss is simply a great guy? He asks you and others in the group to join him for happy hour after work and invites employees to his house for dinner. You become part of his social circle. This may be fine, as long as he treats others in your group the same way. He may simply be a gregarious person, and the corporate culture may be such that these activities are normal. But if it's only you who's being invited, watch out. Your coworkers could become resentful and make life hard for you. You might be seen as an apple-polisher or someone with an unfair advantage when it comes to promotions and raises. Or you may find yourself the subject of unfair gossip about the nature of your personal relationship. Think ahead to the potential repercussions if you become too friendly with your boss.

GETTING ALONG WITH YOUR COWORKERS

Whether you work in a small business or a huge corporation, you'll find yourself dealing with an amazing variety of people, and everyone will be expected to get along for the sake of the business. Management, although it realizes that conflict is a fact of business life, has little patience for the problems brought on by personality clashes, misunderstandings, power plays, back stabbing, faultfinding, and interdepartmental civil wars. The reason? Because all of these things drain time and energy away from corporate goals, and that translates into lost profits.

Some typical coworker personality types are described below. As you learn to get along with people in the business world, keep in mind that problems and disagreements can occur among well-meaning people who have different goals or simply see things from a different point of view. If you try to see things from their perspective and give their views and ideas the respect they deserve, you will receive similar treatment in return.

Just as there are typical types of bosses, there are several common types of difficult coworkers. Face it—sooner or later, you'll have to deal with all of them: back stabbers, complainers, know-it-alls, the nice-but-incompetents, office snakes, gossips, busy-bodies, the uninvolved, doomsayers, and meanies. People, of course, are more complex than we'll portray here. But at least you'll have an idea about how to cope with different types and start to understand why they act as they do.

> Tracy, a junior copywriter at an ad agency, reflects, "In the first few months on the job, it's easy to be friendly and get along with everyone. The reality is that everyone becomes themselves after they get to know one another. I doubt there's any way to hide your frustration and unwillingness to do certain things. The one thing that would have helped me was to have thought before I spoke."

When dealing with difficult people, keep in mind the possible underlying reasons that people behave badly at work:

- They need to feel important.
- They need to be liked and accepted.
- They need to control insecurities.
- They need to feel powerful and in control.

Back Stabbers

These can be found in almost any organization. These people are afraid someone is going to look better or move ahead faster. They're easily threatened and see someone else's success as a threat to their own. If you are a target, the back stabber will cut you down to others while staying civil or even friendly with you; it may be months before you catch on that you're being attacked. If you've trusted this person, the hurt can be enormous. How can you spot back stabbers? By noticing how they talk about other people. Are they overly critical, do they spread ugly rumors, do they gloat when someone fails at something?

You can be sure that if they can say such things about your coworkers, they can say them about you if they start to see you as a threat.

> John was told to spend time with Frank to learn the ins and outs of his new job. Frank was helpful and taught John a lot, but he always seemed to leave out a few necessary details. John would then make mistakes, and Frank would come to the rescue and correct them. John finally realized that Frank needed to feel indispensable and important, and he did this by selectively withholding information.

Complainers

They love to take up your time with endless streams of problems with other coworkers, management, the company, and even the world at large. These people see no good in anything or anyone. Complaining gives them a sense of superiority that at least helps them feel a little bit of power. They usually do no real harm, except to take up your time and drag down your spirits—but who needs that? You may have trouble turning off or getting rid of complainers without appearing rude, but at times you may have to say, "I really can't talk to you now—I've got this deadline to meet." They won't be hurt—they'll just move down the hall to the next victim. Of course, you may just want to make them face their endless whining by saying, "It gets me down when you complain so much—I'd be more interested in spending time trying to figure out how we can fix these problems."

Know-it-alls

These people need to feel in perfect control and superior. Some know-it-alls are truly smart, whereas others are trying to look smart even though they're really not. Both types can be hard to deal with because they think their ideas and solutions are the only ones possible.

People who are secure about their abilities usually welcome and encourage others to contribute thoughts and ideas; they know that two heads can be better than one. When know-it-alls get you down, remember that they're simply acting out the need to be respected and admired. It may not make them easier to take, but at least you know it's not because they think you're stupid.

When dealing with this type of person, be careful that your tone of voice or body language doesn't give away your sense of irritation. You can sometimes get know-it-alls closer to reality by asking intelligent, pointed questions about the things they say. If they realize you aren't easily overwhelmed by their great knowledge, they'll tend to tone things down. They may also begin to respect you and treat you more like an equal, which will help both of you get the job done even if the irritations remain.

Nice-but-incompetents

These people are easy to deal with but can cause problems if you have to depend on them in any way. If a receptionist who may be the soul of goodness messes up your calls or forgets to give you a message, you can't help but feel angry. The problem is that you'd feel like a jerk if you expressed that anger toward the employee, so you say nothing. One day, however, the last straw occurs, and you blow up. You feel terrible, and the receptionist feels worse.

To avoid this fatal buildup, try to let the person know immediately of any problems he or she has caused, as gently and as matter-of-factly as you can. You'll have to make yourself do this, because it won't come easy—ultranice people seem to be especially sensitive to criticism. If you offer positive comments at other times, the coworker will know you're being fair.

People who are always agreeable can also make it hard for you to know where you stand. Getting straight answers and realistic schedules can be next to impossible, because such people will do anything to avoid being unpleasant. If you suspect that someone is telling you something that sounds more like wishful thinking than reality, do a little gentle probing. Ask questions in a nonthreatening way to get to the root of that employee's reasoning. Once your coworker realizes that he or she won't hurt your feelings, you'll probably get the answers you need.

These people also hate to make decisions and can stall projects and plans if they play a key role. When you are in a low-level position, it's just about impossible to encourage them to make the decision that will let you keep going. You can try to discuss the problem with them, but if they balk or try to ignore you, you may want to mention that you'll have to get your boss involved. This may do the trick. If it doesn't, then see your boss.

Office Snakes

These people will do anything to get ahead. They will think nothing of blaming you for their inability to get the job done. They'll gleefully tell your boss about the big goof you made with the client last week. If they catch you in a small error, they'll make sure everyone knows that your work can't be trusted. In the meantime, they're spinning yarns to make themselves look good, and they aren't above reading your mail to find out what's going on. They simply love to start turf battles and aren't happy unless they have someone they can put down. Their superiority as a human being, they seem to believe, excuses them from the demands of ethical behavior that of course apply to everyone else.

It's tempting to try to ignore these people. You think, "Doesn't management see how they operate?" Eventually management probably will, but perhaps not for a long time. Such people have an amazing ability to gain the trust of their superiors. In the meantime, you're getting sideswiped unfairly, and you must protect yourself. As soon as you suspect you're being trampled on, confront the coworker directly, as calmly as you can. Tell the person what you've heard. You'll probably get a denial or be told there was a misunderstanding, but don't argue further—just let it go. By being so direct, you've probably stemmed any future problems. If they continue, however, then go to your boss with all the evidence you can gather. You'll need facts, not hearsay. If a coworker or coworkers have direct knowledge of any attacks against you, let your boss know that you have witnesses. At this point, the productivity and morale of the office is at stake, and the problem now belongs to the boss as well.

Gossips

They love to know everything that's going on with everybody, presumably because it gives them a feeling of power. These people are easy to spot. They'll be the first to ask you all sorts of questions about your personal life, and then they'll share with you the latest news about people you both know. Be careful what you say to someone like this—don't reveal anything you don't want the world to know.

Gossips aren't necessarily women. In fact, some of the worst office gossips are men, but since rumormongering is not expected of them, they seem to get away with it for a while. George, who was a friendly, open kind of guy, carried his propensity for gossip a little too far. During a slow period gossipwise, George spread the word that the company president was due to retire soon. In fact, the president had no such plans. When the rumor reached the president, he confronted the gossipmeister, who admitted his guilt. Needless to say, George was fired on the spot.

Busybodies

They are closely related to gossips, with the added annoyance of wanting to get too involved in your personal life. They want to

> Stephanie recalls, "There were two women in my office who were known to be close friends. The funny thing was that they'd talk about each other to the same people! We could never let on to Pat what Gina had said about her, and we couldn't tell Gina what Pat had said about her. It got confusing after a while, trying to keep things straight."

know all about your love life, your family life, and of course any problems you may be having. Then they'll want to help you solve them. Such people are sometimes quick to take advantage of others as well. For example, you offer to drive a coworker home during a bad storm one night, and she begins to ask for a ride every night. You have to be nice but firm with such people, and tell them you'd rather not—whether it's sharing details of your personal life or doing repeated favors.

The Uninvolved

These are people who stay in the background and try hard to avoid being pulled into projects or events. They figure they can't fail at something if they don't get involved in the first place. You can usually ignore these people until you need their help with something. The best way to get their cooperation is to stay as nonthreatening as possible. Play down the importance of what you're asking them to do. Tell them you'll help in any way you can. Do what you have to do to make them say yes.

Many uninvolved people are really just shy or insecure. When you need their cooperation, try to explain to them why their expertise is important to you. You'll be giving them the assurance they need to come out of their shell. Other people, however, simply don't care about their job and could not care less about helping you; they live for quitting time. There's not much you can do about these people, except to try hard to get along without them—they're career killers.

Doomsayers

They love to predict the worst. The proposal doesn't have a chance, that idea didn't work four years ago and certainly won't work now, the company's competition is too stiff to beat, and on and on. Like complainers, doomsayers feel a sense of power when they make these negative statements. Since they feel that they are incapable of making a positive contribution themselves, they don't wish to see others succeed. They especially love it when people seem to take them seriously and even repeat their dire predictions to others as if they were fact. If the company is facing layoffs, these people are in heaven, so to speak. They'll actually take joy in telling you that your entire department is slated to be cut.

Doomsayers can make you miserable—avoid them whenever you can. Like complainers, they can always find an attentive audience among other dissatisfied employees.

Meanies

They are impossible to deal with. Some just seem to be born mean. They take joy in creating problems for other people. Presumably this gives them a sense of power and control they can't get otherwise. When meanies try to get the best of you, don't give them the satisfaction. If you stand up to them, they'll respect you for it (though they'll never say so) and probably leave you alone in the future. They'd rather spend their time on people who are easier to intimidate.

Julie, a public relations assistant, says, "Some meanies hate their jobs but don't have the confidence to go out and find a better job. They're miserable, and they'd like everyone around them to be miserable as well. Don't ever ask a meanie to help you on a project—you'll just be asking for trouble."

It may help you to cope if you think of meanies as sad people who live shallow lives. If a meanie creates a real problem for you that you can't seem to work out yourself, talk to your boss about it. People like this can be destructive at times, but mostly they stick to the small stuff—they don't have the courage to do truly evil things.

Some people think that the only way they can accomplish anything is to bully someone into it. On the plus side, if you can cope with someone like this, you'll earn the eternal admiration of coworkers who have had similar problems with the meanie.

DEALING WITH DIFFICULT PEOPLE IN GENERAL

Why is it so hard to get along with some people? There are two basic reasons: (1) the obvious fact that individuals have unique combinations of personality, background, and goals; and (2) the difficulty we all have in "reading" other people and being "read" correctly ourselves. Remember the truism that it's hard to see ourselves as others see us? The problem is that we tend to judge the actions and motives of others from our own point of view. But the secret is to try to see the situation through the eyes of the other person.

Here's an example. Jack was unhappy with the way Joel, who managed the Accounting Department, was processing his invoices each month. He got along with Joel fairly well, so one day Jack decided to drop by and voice his complaints. His intention was to do this in a noncritical, matter-of-fact way, in the hope that Joel would investigate the problem and find a solution.

To Jack's surprise, Joel quickly got defensive. He claimed that Jack's complaints had no basis in fact and suggested that he was just trying to cause trouble where none existed. Jack hardly knew what to say, but he realized that he'd reached an impasse. What happened here?

It turned out that Joel was also under fire from several other managers who had similar complaints, which Jack had no knowledge of. Joel's manager was aware of the bosses' dissatisfaction and had just issued Joel an ultimatum to improve his performance soon or be fired. Jack's unannounced visit caught Joel unprepared during a time of great stress, and the only way he could cope with the problem was to deny it. Denial and blame are two frequent sources of workplace difficulties, because they provide a way for people to feel better without having to face the real problem.

In this case, Jack had no way of knowing about Joel's other problems. He could have become angry with Joel and thus added another level of conflict to the situation. But instead he "read" that Joel wasn't in a rational frame of mind, for whatever reason, and left the room. Later Jack asked some other managers if they had experienced any problems with Joel, and eventually he was able to piece together the whole story. At that point he knew that he wasn't the only person with a complaint and decided to wait things out for a while before saying anything further.

Human Nature at Work

It's a basic fact of business life that people want to feel competent in their jobs and to believe that they are an important part of the organization. If they find themselves in a job that is beyond their capabilities, or they feel ignored and unappreciated, they may act in ways that rub us the wrong way but that help them cope with a sense of inadequacy and lack of power. This may sound terribly psychological, but understanding human nature is key to getting along at work. Sometimes you have to look beyond the surface to understand people and their actions. For any puzzling or frustrating human act, there are probably several possible reasons behind it. Try to come up with a least a few of them before you assume anything.

If you have an ongoing problem with a coworker, it's best to get it out in the open rather than remain silent and let the situation get worse. Sit down face-to-face, and talk in a way that is unaccusing, matter-of-fact, and professional. Rid your voice of any anger or criticism. Don't do this by memo or E-mail. State the problem, and, if appropriate, ask the person for his or her point of view. Be sure to listen attentively, without interrupting. Then ask the coworker to hear out your side. If things turn unpleasant, leave the room rather than escalate the tension—in other words, don't let the other person get your goat and make you say or do things you'll regret later.

Even if you feel you didn't cause the problem, you may have to be the one to reach out to fix it. The goal should be to clear the air, not to lay the blame and suffer in silence. Not only is it the mature and professional thing to do, but you can save yourself from the stress that results from unresolved conflicts. If for no other reason, try to settle the difficulty for your own peace of mind.

If your efforts fail, think about finding an impartial person to serve as a mediator. Often a third party can break down barriers and open up lines of communication. In short, try to resolve conflicts in any way you can, before they reflect on your performance and your good reputation.

Leigh and Susan, who were cubicle mates, had the same job title but Susan had been with the company longer. Every time Leigh would ask Susan a question, she would get a sarcastic, demeaning response. Leigh wasn't sure whether Susan felt threatened by her presence or just enjoyed feeling superior. Leigh thought about complaining to their boss about the problem but instead decided to confront Susan directly. The next time it happened, Leigh quietly said, "You know, it hurts when you say things like 'I'm surprised you don't know this,' and I wish you'd stop." Amazingly, Susan hadn't consciously realized what she was doing and apologized to Leigh immediately. The comments and responses ceased after that. It takes a little bit of nerve to be so direct, but in the long run a few minutes of discomfort can prevent the big problems that result from stored-up anger and resentment.

Learn to Negotiate, Not Fight

In the business world, like it or not, the only people that can always have their way are the people in charge—and even they must often bend to the wishes of a board of directors or the stockholders. Everyone else must learn to compromise and negotiate for his or her own best interests. There's a difference between standing your ground for something you deeply believe in and standing your ground for a method or an idea that is one of several that would work. To disagree and be stubborn just because you want things to go your way is to invite disaster. People will avoid you and stop asking for your contributions.

Keep these points in mind whenever you need to negotiate with someone. First, make sure both of you are absolutely clear on the problem or issue under discussion. This may sound like a silly thing to do, but you'd be surprised at how often people will argue for hours on a subject, only to find out later that they were talking about two different things! Don't assume anything. Start out by stating exactly what you think the issue is and ask your colleague if she agrees; better yet, ask her to state her understanding as well. In the process, you may find some side issues that will also need to be addressed.

Next, agree on the outcome you'd both like to see. Let's say the problem is late reporting of sales results. Is the solution to find new software for entering orders and sales into the computer, or is the goal to simply shave some time off the data entry process? Unless the two of you agree on the end result, you may be heading in different directions.

Then list all the facts relating to the problem. It may help to write them on a whiteboard or on flipsheets so you can refer to them as necessary. If the other person stays silent, ask her to contribute or at least agree with what's being said—you don't want her waiting until the very end of the discussion to offer new information that changes everything.

Try hard to take a positive attitude. Keep in mind that the purpose of your discussion is to come up with a solution, not to discredit the other person or have your way. Contain any anger that may surface, and try your best to stay calm and businesslike. Let the other person talk and don't interrupt. If you must disagree, wait until she's said her piece. Then ask for the same courtesy on her part when you wish to talk. If you don't understand something, ask questions to be sure her point of view is clear to you. Stay focused on the problem and avoid making critical comments.

Sometimes a self-deprecating manner can defuse a tense situation. Humor, especially if used at the right time, can help put things in perspective. Even taking the blame, if appropriate, can help open up roadblocks to the final solution.

Finally, recognize that you don't always have to be right, and that in fact you may not be right. Other people have much to offer, and they are more likely to be committed to achieving the end result if they feel they had a voice in deciding it.

The Problem with Perfectionism

Misguided perfectionism—either your own or a coworker's—can be the source of many conflicts. For example, typographical errors in memos and reports drive some people to total distraction, while others simply consider them a normal occurrence. Often the problem is that some people have such rigid personalities that, to them, a typo in a memo read by four people takes on the same importance as the misspelling of the president's name in the corporate brochure. To such people, the world is black and white, with no room for gray areas, different approaches, or differences of opinion.

Chris explains how he dealt with the "my way is best" problem: "No matter how you did something, Chuck would tell you how he'd do it, implying that his way was better. But that's not all. If you used the number pad on your keyboard, he'd tell you to use the top row instead. If you used the top row, he'd tell you to use the number pad. I guess he just liked to have his say. After a while I learned to nod politely and ignore his recommendations."

Many difficult people will want you to adopt their standards and their methods because they are so sure that their way is right. If your boss is such a person, it's best, for now anyway, to do things his way. If the person is a coworker, you simply need to stand your ground. Explaining your point of view may work, but more likely you'll just have to say, "I prefer to do it this way."

Being flexible means adjusting your goals and attitudes to fit the situation at hand; it doesn't necessarily mean you are without standards or principles. In the name of perfectionism, some people will devote the same amount of time and energy to minor problems as to major ones. Doing good work is important, but doing the right work at the right time with the right level of effort is even more so.

If You Really Get Angry

Controlling your anger at work is extremely important. Once you've lost your cool and said or done things you can't take back, you've labeled yourself as a difficult person, to be avoided at all costs. Relationships and reputations have been destroyed by outbursts lasting only a few seconds. When you are at the beginning of your career, you need to be especially careful not to display a lack of control. You could earn a reputation that could follow you for a long time. In the short term, it could even get you fired.

Instead of blowing up, learn to bite your tongue or count to ten. Accept the fact that dealing with others is often difficult and that disagreement is a normal part of business life. Don't take negative comments personally, even if they hurt for a while. Some people have been known to let a misguided remark affect their job performance. The bottom line is this: Why should you give a difficult person that kind of power over your life?

Some people try to get even by putting down others behind their backs. In some offices, this is an unofficial sport. People who take joy in reporting on the foibles and mistakes of their colleagues waste company time and cast a pall over the office. They like to demean and criticize others because it makes them feel superior and important; their energies would be better spent trying to *become* a superior kind of person, rather than tear down others in order to boost their own self-confidence. Don't let it happen to you.

Don't Compare Yourself with Others

If you want to make yourself miserable, start comparing yourself with other people in your office. Note how your boss treats your coworkers, and get concerned if she seems to favor one person in particular. Feel stupid if Jill understands the word processing program better than you do (and never mind that she's been using it for five years). Feel inefficient if Mark can whip out his weekly report in an hour, but it still takes you three.

It's only natural to use others as a gauge for judging your own competence—after all, you've just been through almost two decades of school, where comparisons were a fact of life (think about the practice of grading on the curve!). But you can quickly get demoralized in your first job by thinking you have to be as good as the people who have been there much longer than you. Give yourself a break, and don't be afraid to ask what you think are stupid questions. People will respect you for caring, and you'll be surprised at the support you'll receive.

If you come in with the attitude that you already know it all, your boss and your coworkers will be amused at first, then irritated. You won't make any friends, and when you finally do call for help, it may not be there.

The workplace may seem competitive and it often is, come promotion time. Managers look to promote people who are sure of themselves and their abilities, who show a desire to continue growing and learning, and who can cooperate with others. The person you need to worry about surpassing is yourself.

· 5 ·

Integrity at Work

*I*ntegrity—sounds like one of those lofty words that have no bearing on everyday life, doesn't it? In fact, it's a quality, either in a person or an organization, that is crucial to long-term, solid success.

What does *integrity* mean? Some synonyms are *honesty, trustworthiness, fairness, loyalty, sincerity,* and *consistency.* A dictionary definition is "moral soundness, steadfastness of purpose, responsibility, or trust."

Integrity is unfortunately so rare in business and politics these days that a person who truly possesses it stands out—think about how people feel about Colin Powell. People with integrity know what they believe in, and they act on what they think is right, regardless of the consequences. They don't say one thing and do another. They don't believe one thing today and the opposite tomorrow unless there's a good reason to change their mind. They don't lie, cut corners, or make promises they know they can't keep. You can count on them to do what they say they'll do. People like this are a pleasure to work with and do business with.

A 1996 survey found that the single most important characteristic of successful business leaders was honesty, but in the business world, job *competence* is also a factor in integrity. Some people are honest and trustworthy but are not able to carry out the duties of their job. Their unreliability in this regard makes it hard for others to count on them, even if their intentions are good.

If you want to be known as a person of integrity—

- You'll take full responsibility for the actions and decisions you make.
- You won't blame others for your mistakes or misjudgments.
- You won't make excuses or rationalizations.
- You'll keep all promises and commitments, even those that seem small and insignificant.
- You won't take shortcuts.
- You won't lie to or mislead people.
- You'll act consistently, even courageously, in carrying out your beliefs; people will be able to predict how you'll act.
- You'll do the best job you know how, and you won't fake doing work that is beyond your capabilities.
- Finally, when deciding how to act or what to do, you'll do what you believe is deep-down right and not take the easy way out.

The next section gives some examples of thoughts and actions that demonstrate a lack of integrity.

RIGHT OR WRONG?

"No one will care if I take a few packages of these Post-its home—the company buys them by the thousands."

Many companies have had to restrict access to their supply rooms because employees were outfitting their home offices and kids' rooms with company office supplies. The losses were so great that it was cheaper to hire a full-time person to hand out supplies than to bear the expense of this seemingly innocent form of employee theft. Taking something that's not yours is theft, no matter how small the item. Theft includes personal use of the company's postage meter, fax machine (for long-distance faxes), and copy machine. Make sure you find out company policy on personal use of these items before using them.

Nicole, a technical services recruiter, has a surefire way to screen the number of job applicants she considers: "You'd be surprised at how many people send me résumés with cover letters printed on their current employer's stationery. Some even use their employer's envelopes, postage meter, or fax machine! Regardless of their qualifications, I toss these résumés into the trash can the minute I see them. I couldn't trust someone who would take advantage of an employer that way."

"We can have that product to you in two weeks,
guaranteed, if you'll place your order today."

It's the end of the quarter and Brady needs to meet his quota or he won't get a bonus. He knows that the product in question is about a month from being ready to ship to customers, but that doesn't stop him from pulling out all the stops to make a sale. "It's just another couple of weeks," he rationalizes. "If they call me in two weeks to complain that it hasn't arrived, I'll just tell them that a few unexpected problems came up at the factory. By then, what else can they do but wait?"

Making promises you know you can't keep is just about the worst thing you can do to your career and to yourself. Sometimes the reason is not deliberate deception but simply the desire not to upset anyone. Making such promises may work once, but it rarely works twice—people will stop believing anything you say.

"Sure, I sent that report to Mr. Smith yesterday,
just like you asked." (If I send it by overnight mail today,
he'll never know the difference.)

Most bosses seem to have a sixth sense about these things. You might get away with one or two small lies, but after a while they'll catch up with you. In the example above, let's say Mr. Smith calls your boss to thank him for sending the report, mentioning that it wasn't so urgent that it had to be sent via overnight mail. Your boss distinctly remembers telling you to use regular mail. He puts two and two together and suspects you were trying to cover up your forgetfulness. The irony is that the mistake itself, if owned up to, would have been quickly forgiven and forgotten. Now your boss feels he's been lied to. Can he trust anything you say? This is how small problems can lead to big ones.

Saying what you think others *want* to hear may make you and them feel better for the moment, but the loss of trust that eventually results isn't worth the temporary good feelings. It's best to be up front with people, even if it hurts a little at the time.

"The boss left early today—so it's okay
if I cut out at four-thirty instead of five."

It was four o'clock and Kristin's boss had just left for the day. "I'll wait awhile and then get out of here," Kristin said to herself. At four-thirty, she headed for the parking lot, only to run into her boss, who was talking with another manager near the exit. Now Kristin's boss is not sure what Kristin might do when she's not around.

If your desk is not visible from your boss's office, you may get away with arriving late, leaving early, or taking long breaks and long lunches for awhile, but eventually your behavior will catch up with you. If your boss drops by your desk once or twice a day and you're not there half the time, she'll begin to wonder. Worse, she may begin to check on you more often.

Dependability is important, and your boss is frustrated that you're not around when she needs you. She's also angry that you don't seem to understand that the company is paying you for hours you're not working.

"I need to take the rest of the week off—my grandmother died."

Some people have an amazing number of grandmothers pass away over the course of a career. Others have Friday headaches, Monday stomachaches, and all-day dental appointments. Some career advice books suggest that it's okay to take a mental health day every so often on the pretext of being ill. But unless you're a proficient liar, most bosses can tell a real illness or emergency from a made-up one. Is it worth planting a seed of distrust in your boss's mind for a day or two off?

Many employees think that sick leave days are like vacation days—that they're there for you to take, even if you're not ill. In fact, most companies don't expect that the average employee will use every sick leave day. These absences are meant to be taken when you are truly too ill to come in to work.

If you need the time off, be forthright about it and request it. Offer to take it without pay if you must. Most people understand and will respect you for not making up lame excuses.

> *"I've got to finish this job by the close of business—there just*
> *won't be time to double-check a few of those numbers.*
> *I'm sure they're okay—I'll do it next time for sure."*

When schedules are tight, it's easy to rationalize skipping steps or taking shortcuts. If you're bored or unmotivated, it's also easy to do the least you can get away with. As with many of the other examples in this chapter, this attitude will catch up with you sooner or later. By then, you will have branded yourself as someone whose work can't always be counted on. It's so important in your first year to do the very best job you can. If you don't, you may not be first choice for any promotions, cross-training programs, or raises. Your boss will be able to spot sloppy work or a haphazard approach very quickly—don't underestimate him.

> *"The great thing about the Internet is that it's so easy*
> *to keep up with my friends from college. Even better,*
> *everyone thinks I'm working away at my computer!"*

The Internet has surpassed computer games as one of the biggest time wasters in business today. If your company has provided you with Internet access for business purposes, be sure you don't abuse the benefit. If you would like to get on the Internet during lunch or after work hours, check with your boss—it may be okay. Just be up front about it.

"I'll just eat the free snacks at the bar and
claim a $20 dinner on my expense report—I could
sure use the extra cash this month."

Expense-report cheating is probably the most common form of corporate theft. In fact, it's so commonplace that many employees believe it's okay to stretch things because they know they won't get caught. But it's cheating, nevertheless.

Some people do things that they probably don't consider cheating. For example, David, a bachelor, takes all his dirty shirts and suits with him on a three-day business trip and sends them to the hotel cleaners. The charge is buried in his hotel bill, where it is unlikely to be picked up unless someone looks closely.

Joe took his girlfriend on a business trip to California, where they spent a few extra days sightseeing in the rental car Joe charged to the company account. He didn't pay for the days of personal use out of his own pocket because he figured no one would catch the added time. If renting the car for a few extra days qualified Joe for a lower weekly rate, it might be okay, especially if the total charge is lower than for the shorter period. Whatever you do, it's best to tell your boss—or whoever approves your expense report—about your plans, so that no misunderstandings occur.

"Mom, here's my company's 800 number—
call me anytime on it."

Many companies keep a close eye on personal phone calls because so many employees spend hours each week making them. Long-distance calls are an even bigger problem because of the expense involved. Most employees know that if they make a long-distance call from their desk phone, the call will appear on the monthly bill, showing their extension, the number called, and the time and length of the call. To avoid being caught, they give their friends and relatives the company's toll-free number, which rings in at the switchboard just like any other call.

What they don't realize is (1) the call is not toll-free to the company, which must pay a monthly service charge *and* a per call charge that is usually higher than a regular long-distance call; and (2) the calls are itemized on the monthly bill, so that the manager can see where they're coming from and the length of each call. The volume of calls may be so high that you'd never get caught, but you never know. Regardless, it's not right to use company time, equipment, and services for personal reasons, unless your boss has told you otherwise. Some companies have a relaxed attitude toward personal use of long-distance services, however, so you may want to find out for sure.

Most businesses accept the fact that their employees will need to conduct some personal business during the day and don't mind the time spent on a few short calls. But if the privilege is abused—say, you plan your entire wedding from your desk—people will be upset. Even if your boss doesn't catch you, your office mates will surely notice. Don't think they won't resent your slacking off if they're trying to work—they will. And don't be surprised if they complain about it—perhaps even to your boss.

> *"I promised Sue I would keep this to myself, but*
> *I know she wouldn't mind if I tell you."*

Some news and information is so juicy that some people can't resist the urge to pass it on. If you do this often enough, eventually people will believe that you can't be trusted to keep your mouth shut.

Would you trust someone who betrayed a confidence? You'd probably think twice before confiding in someone who has passed along such information to you. And if you think it's okay because the person you tell is a close friend, you may want to think again. Friendships in the business world have been known to change overnight. Your innermost fears and secrets could be public knowledge if something happened between you.

It's possible that your boss may share certain information with you as a test of your ability to keep things to yourself. If she says something like "Just between you and me . . . ," take it to mean that she doesn't want the information passed on. If it comes back to her in a few days, she'll know it came from you. In some businesses, a person's ability to protect confidential information is critical, and any lapses may be grounds for dismissal.

"Rob, that's a great idea. I'm surprised
no one has thought of it before."

Well . . . in fact, Rob sort of "borrowed" the idea from a coworker who had been brainstorming with his friends one day at lunch. Rob was at the next table and overheard the conversation. He just couldn't resist sharing the idea with his boss, who had been struggling with a problem that the idea would fix. How could Rob admit that the idea wasn't really his? Besides, he didn't even know the name of the employee whose idea it was.

Rob may get away with this, and he may not. The bigger problem is that he's knowingly taking credit for something that wasn't his, and he'll have to live with this knowledge.

Josh, a marketing assistant, says, "When I get credited for working on something that another person also helped out on, I'll say something like 'Well, I can't take all the credit—John put in lots of hours, too.' This keeps everything straight. If you take credit when you shouldn't, it's like lying. I can sleep at night knowing I'm as truthful as I can be, and besides, I don't have to worry about someone wanting to stab me in the back. I've found that bosses sometimes will test you on this 'taking credit where it's not due' thing."

MORAL DILEMMAS

Sooner or later you'll find yourself in a sticky situation because of someone else's behavior. Knowing what to do can be difficult, if only because of your inexperience and low status in the organization. You may want to make a stand or right a wrong, but you may fear that you'll jeopardize your job and even your career. There are no easy answers to any of the following situations. You will have to search your conscience and draw on your own moral strength and values to find answers.

The Fictional Time Sheet

Jodie worked for a large high-tech company that held several important contracts with the federal government. Each week she had to complete a time sheet that showed the hours she worked on each contract. Her company used that information to bill the government, so it was important that the information be accurate; the company could lose the contract if it falsified hours in any way.

Jodie's boss came to her one day and told her to write in four hours of overtime on her time sheet for a particular day that week. He said she wouldn't get paid any more than she normally did because she was a salaried, not an hourly, employee. He offered no explanation for his request but made it clear that she had no choice in the matter.

Jodie was fairly sure that if she added those four hours, her company would bill the government for that time at overtime rates. She knew it wasn't right, but she didn't think she could disobey her boss. Rather than risk incurring her boss's anger and possibly lose her job, she did as she was told. What could she have done instead?

She might have said something like this: "Sam, as I understand it, I'm personally responsible for the accuracy of my time sheet. I really have a problem with putting down information I know is not correct. I wish you wouldn't put me in this situation."

Sam most likely would back off rather than force the issue. After all, he wouldn't want to make things worse by trying to pressure Jodie. It's possible that Sam doesn't like the idea either, but was told by his boss to increase the hours.

Jodie's second moral dilemma is whether to report her boss's actions to someone else in the company. If she goes to Sam's boss, and it turns out that he was the one who instructed Sam to beef up the hours, Jodie would be seen as someone who could create difficulties for everyone. But he would also know that if he fired her, she would have grounds for a wrongful-dismissal lawsuit against the company. On the other hand, Sam's boss may be appalled to find out what is going on and appreciate Jodie's courage.

Some larger companies have telephone hot lines that encourage employees to report, anonymously, any unethical or illegal business practices they've witnessed. If Jodie's company has such a line, she should call it. An alternative would be for her to speak to someone in the Contracts or Human Resources Department. She is in the unfortunate situation of knowing about something that could jeopardize the company's ability to do business with one of its largest customers. She may like her boss and not want to get him in trouble, but her first loyalty belongs to her company as a whole (not to mention to her own ethical values).

Also known as a "whistle-blower" line, a company's telephone hot line may be used to get advice or guidance on business ethics in general. If you see or hear of anything that is questionable, you should feel free to use the hot line to get help or advice.

A similar situation sometimes arises in law firms and consulting companies, where employees must record hours worked for each client. These hours serve as the basis for billing the client. The firm may specify strict guidelines; for example, paralegals may be told to spend 90 percent of their time on billable work, with only 10 percent on general administrative duties. If they fall short during the week, they may find it tempting to "pad" their time sheets with extra client hours so that they don't look bad to their bosses.

Or, as in the example given earlier, the boss may tell employees to add, to certain client accounts, hours not actually worked. Again, it will be difficult for the employee to refuse, but the alternative is to knowingly engage in illegal or unethical acts.

Witness to Deceit

After you've been on the job for almost a year, you begin to notice that your department's sales figures don't seem quite right. You start double-checking entries and finally come to the realization that your boss is manipulating the numbers to make things look better than they are. What do you do?

You realize your suspicions could be wrong; you haven't been with the company that long, and there could be another explanation for the disparity. Yet after a second look, it seems clear that your boss is the problem. You don't want to go to *her* boss and get her fired, but you don't feel it's right to remain silent.

Your best bet is to mention casually to your boss that the figures are puzzling to you and you'd like an explanation so that you can better understand them. At this point, you can hope she provides a logical reason. But if your suspicions turn out to be true, she'll realize you're on to her and either brush you off or invent some elaborate and incomprehensible explanation. Then all you can do is hope she later corrects the figures because she knows she might get caught. (After all, *you* caught her, and you haven't been around that long.) If you decide to challenge her further or go to her boss, you will risk your own job. It's a decision you'll have to make depending on your circumstances and the seriousness of the deception.

Loose Lips

An old friend from college who works for a competitor of your company calls one day to invite you to lunch. You go and have a great time reminiscing about school and catching up on news of mutual friends. Soon the conversation turns to work, and before you realize it, your friend is asking you some fairly specific questions about your company's plans. In your position, you aren't privy to many details, so you figure there's no harm in answering his general questions. As you head back to the office, though, you have an uneasy feeling—did you say too much?

You may have. It's best to feign ignorance or just say you aren't able to talk about certain things. Since you may not understand the relevance of the information being sought, you won't know if you say something that could hurt your company. Even a fact that seems insignificant to you may be of real importance to an outsider. Don't take the chance.

If you take a phone call from someone who asks pointed questions about your company's finances or business plans or processes, try to find out as much as you can about the person, and then refuse to answer any questions until you can check with your boss. Just say something like "I'll have to get back to you on that." The person on the other end may be a competitor trying to gather facts and figures or an attorney trying to get background information for a lawsuit you may have no knowledge of. Callers seeking references on former employees should *always* be routed to your Human Resources Department.

Customers will sometimes try to find out how your company arrives at prices; they may ask about overhead percentages and similar proprietary information, and they may figure you'll be naive enough to spill the beans. Don't do it. Again, you're in an ideal situation to say, "I really don't know—let me check with my boss."

If you signed an employment contract when you were hired, take a look at it. There's probably a clause that states you will not reveal trade secrets or proprietary information about the company, either directly or indirectly. Companies are serious about this one; profits and competitive stance are at stake.

The Overly Friendly Vendor

If your job requires you to deal with outside suppliers—called vendors in most businesses—you should check with your Contracts or Procurement Department for company guidelines on the topic. Most companies have specific and strict rules about accepting gifts, meals, or other items of monetary value from vendors.

Elizabeth was excited when a computer salesman offered her two tickets to a sold-out football play-off game in their city. All he asked was for her to encourage her boss to buy the system he was selling. She felt sure that her boss was going to approve the purchase anyway, but she felt a twinge of guilt, knowing that she was getting something for herself out of the deal. What should she have done?

Elizabeth should have politely declined the salesman's offer of tickets, saying simply that she wasn't allowed to accept any form of gift from vendors. This advice applies whether or not your company has explicit rules on vendor gifts—it's just smart to avoid the appearance of impropriety, no matter how small the gift.

If your company does work for government agencies, you should be aware that, in regard to giving gifts to federal workers, strict rules often apply to items or meals over a certain value. The current limit on gifts to government employees is five dollars, for example. Check with your boss or your contracts office before giving anything to a government employee; don't even offer to pay for the person's lunch.

LITTLE THINGS MEAN A LOT

Integrity does not result from one courageous act but rather from many small acts, consistently performed over time. Keeping a promise to return a phone call by the next morning is as important as bringing in an entire project on schedule. If you do as you say some of the time but not all of the time, you are not a person of integrity. Because of your inconsistency, people cannot trust you.

This approach sounds hard to put into practice. But is it? Think about the tension and stress you create for yourself by telling small lies. It's hard to remember what you said to different people, and there's always the chance you'll get caught. The stress this can create in your life can be great. Consider the disappointment you cause when your promises fall through. It's difficult to develop solid and satisfying working relationships with people who aren't sure they can count on you.

It's true that many people who take shortcuts, mislead, deceive, and generally have little respect for others succeed in the business world. But sooner or later their actions catch up with them. They've also ruined many relationships along the way, and it's hard to imagine that they can live with a clear conscience.

Many managers believe that it's better to be respected than to be popular. Think about it—would you rather have a boss who treats you fairly and honestly even if it hurts at times, or one who tells you what you want to hear but goes back on his or her promise to promote you?

True success is not measured by title and salary alone. Rather, it's knowing that you have worked with other people in a way *you* can be proud of, and that you've earned their respect and trust. This is a reputation worth striving for, and it is earned one small act at a time.

6

Getting the Job Done

$\mathbf{A}$nyone in a new job needs at least six months to start to feel comfortable in it, so don't be surprised if you feel overwhelmed at first. Every job, whether it's your first or your fifth, has its own special challenges that will take awhile to master. But if you can learn a few of the basic skills needed for almost any job—to control and organize paperwork, manage your time, and work with and through others—you'll be well ahead of most people. This chapter will explain the techniques that will help you work smarter and faster.

HOW TO GET ORGANIZED

Most important to being organized is how well you control the many pieces of your job, from managing time and information to managing tasks and projects. Here we'll discuss several proven tools and techniques for staying in control.

Keeping a Calendar

The first tool you'll need to organize your work life is a calendar you can carry around with you (to meetings and customer visits, for example). While you're at your desk, you should keep it open to the current day or week. The best kind are the spiral-bound week-at-a-time calendars that give you plenty of room for notes for each day. Computer versions are available and can provide some nifty automatic features. But unless you keep the program on a laptop computer that you carry with you everywhere, an electronic calendar won't be as portable and as easy to refer to and revise as a paper calendar.

Think of your calendar as a way to back up your own, sometimes faulty, memory. Once you get into your job, you'll find out how hard it is to keep track of promises made, due dates, meeting times, and even lunch plans. The idea is to write down *everything* that you can't trust to memory. Here are a few examples:

• Your boss wants a monthly inventory report from you by the fifth of each month. Take out your calendar right now and jot down reminders ("inventory report due the 5th") on February 1, March 1, and so on, to get it done. (For recurring tasks with easy-to-remember dates like the first of the month, you probably won't need the calendar reminders after the first few months.)

• One of your suppliers promises to deliver an item by May 22. Go to that day in your calendar and write yourself a reminder to expect delivery.

• Your boss has called a staff meeting for ten o'clock next Wednesday in the second floor conference room. Jot down the time and place right now in your calendar, not on a slip of paper that could get lost.

• You've promised your boss that you'll complete a project in sixty days. Agree on the actual date—let's say October 10—and then write it down in the calendar. Write a reminder in the block for October 1 that the due date is approaching.

• You've been given deadlines for applying for health insurance, a 401(k) plan, or similar programs. Write reminders on those due dates, as well as on dates a few days ahead of the deadline, to give yourself time to complete any paperwork.

• Note when your next performance review is due.

More than any other single tool, your desk calendar will help you keep promises, stay on top of changing situations, and generally keep you out of trouble. Having all these important dates and times written down will also relieve you of the stress that would result if you tried to keep everything in your head.

If you have several projects you must keep track of, you may want to transfer important milestone dates to a large wall calendar. This will let you see the month at a glance and help you manage conflicts and busy periods. For example, let's say you're committed to working the last five days of the month on an important client proposal and around the middle of the month a coworker asks you to pick up her duties on two of those days. You look at your calendar and see that you couldn't possibly do both. It's much better to say no early on, when people have time to explore other options, than to let them down later.

Managing Paper

For years people have predicted that computers would result in a paperless work environment, but the reality is that there's more paper than ever. Managing the flow and organization of paper is a job you'll need to master. Let's start with the desk and file cabinets you inherited.

See What You Have. In your first few days on the job, take a close look at the contents of your desk and file drawers. Pull out files one at a time and flip through them to see what's there. Most of it won't have any relevance for you yet, but at least you can get familiar with the kinds of paperwork you're likely to continue seeing. While you're doing this, throw out any outdated information you know you won't need, such as brochures announcing programs of two years ago or memos inviting people to meetings that have already happened. Depending on how efficient your predecessor was, you may not find too much that you can safely throw out just now. In about six months you can go back and really clean up. By then you'll know whether someone else in the office keeps files of the same documents and whether you're likely to need certain files in the future.

Check shelves and other storage areas to see what's there. Throw out old phone books, out-of-date catalogs, and any other obviously unneeded items. If you have any questions about whether to keep something, ask your boss or coworkers.

Manage the Flow. Now let's look at the paper you're receiving and creating. You probably won't be getting a lot of mail in your first job, but it's a good time to form efficient habits for dealing with paper. The first rule of thumb is to try not to handle a piece of paper more than once or twice at the most. As something crosses your desk, you should classify it into one of three categories: (1) read it and pitch it; (2) read it and act on it; or (3) read it and file it for future reference.

In the first category you'll have memos inviting you to meetings (which you'll immediately write down in your desk calendar), announcements of things like fire alarm test schedules and company ski trips, and plain old junk mail. There's no need to keep such things, so make notes in your calendar of anything important and toss the pieces of paper. Other items that fall into this category are trade magazines, newsletters, and newspapers (although you may want to keep certain issues or certain articles). Some of these items will be too lengthy for you to read at the time, so set them aside for your lunch hour or put them in your bag or briefcase to take home and read.

The second category is the most important. If you can act on something quickly, then do it right away—simple things like making a phone call or placing an order. If the task will take longer than a few minutes, put the piece of paper in a file folder or box labeled "To Do." We'll come back to this file later.

The third category consists of things like updated phone lists, procedural changes, reports that you'll need to refer to, and similar information of long-term reference value. Put these items in a folder or box labeled "To Be Filed" and plan on filing them once a week. You could file as you go along, but it's probably a little more efficient to do all your filing at once.

Set Up a Filing System. You should follow a few basic rules when you're setting up a file system or revamping an existing one. First, when deciding what to name a folder, use the most generic term possible—the word or term you're most likely to think of when you're searching for something. If you get too specific, the chances are you won't be able to find the file two months later. For example, put all marketing-related papers in a folder called "Marketing" rather than create separate folders for "Mailing List Info" and "Copywriting Tips." Once your marketing file becomes two inches thick, you can think about creating separate files for such topics, and even then you may want to keep the smaller files within a larger (preferably hanging-type) file folder called "Marketing."

Second, don't let your file drawers get so crowded that you have to stuff the folders in. Either ask for another file drawer or ruthlessly clean out what you have. You may even be able to move some files to a storage area—check with your boss.

Third, you will probably want to arrange the folders alphabetically, but some people prefer placing their most frequently used folders at the front of the drawer. Keep in mind that a day will come—you'll be out sick or on vacation—when someone in your office, perhaps your boss, will need to find something you've filed. Try to make it easy for that person to locate the item—you'll make his or her day. You may even want to make a list that notes the names of your files, their locations, and their contents to give to your boss or anyone else who might need to use them when you're away. This list might even help you if you ever forget where you put something.

Fourth, use the available supplies to make it easy and quick to find things. Some people like to color-code their files for quick access. This works as long as you don't have too many colors to keep track of. Note that file folder tabs come in different "cuts" that can be arranged so that one folder doesn't block the label on the file behind it. There's nothing more frustrating than searching for a file that was there all along, just hidden from view.

For frequently referred-to information—say, for a special project you're working on—you may want to use a three-ring binder instead of file folders to organize related papers. Divider tabs can provide quick access, and you can easily add and remove materials that change. Having all the information you need in one volume can be a real boost to efficiency.

Keep Your Desk Clean. You don't have to keep your desk absolutely bare—people will wonder if you have any work to do! But you should attempt to keep clutter to a minimum, if only to make it easier to find information you need. Using folders to organize your work is a start, as described earlier. After a busy day, your desk will probably be overflowing again. Take a few minutes before you go home to sort through the mess and put things in their proper folders, even if you decide to leave the folders on your desk. You'll retain control of your paperwork, and you'll be in a better frame of mind to tackle things in the morning.

TIME MANAGEMENT

It's often said that everyone has the same number of hours in the day to accomplish a job—so why is it that some people seem to get so much more done? Because they know how to set priorities and control interruptions and other time wasters.

Control Interruptions

You'll probably be surprised at how much of your day is spent in conversations and meetings that are not really relevant to getting the job done. Interruptions are probably the most clear and frustrating example of how your day can get away from you. Phone calls, and coworkers who drop by to ask a question or chat, can stretch a thirty-minute task into one that takes all morning. Keep in mind, however, that you should never view calls from customers as interruptions—they're the reason you have a job in the first place!

If you find that it takes forever to get something done because of interruptions, there are a few tactics you can use to regain control of your time. Unfortunately, because of your entry-level status, you probably won't have certain options available to you that managers have—such as the ability to close your door or delegate tasks or hold phone calls. Here are a few things you can do:

- If coworkers drop by your desk, just tell them that you have to get something done by noon or five and ask if you can get back to them when you're through. Don't even let them start talking if you can help it. You probably shouldn't use this approach with your boss or another manager, however.
- It's always best, especially in your position, to answer the phone when it rings rather than let the call go to a secretary or to voice mail. If the caller is long-winded or just wants to chat, say something like "I've got to run now—can I call you back later?" implying that you have an important meeting to go to. If you must let the calls go to voice mail, be sure to return them that day.
- If you have a task that demands your total concentration, see if you can find an empty office or conference room to work in for a few hours. Be sure to let your boss know where you are and what you're doing.
- If you're lucky enough to have a door you can close, close it and put up a sign that says something like "Working on monthly report. Will be through at 11 A.M." You might even ask visitors to write their names on a sheet that says you'll get back to them when you're through.

Be sure not to abuse these tactics. People will expect you to be available most of the time and will be upset if they can never catch you. If you have a door and keep it closed half the time, for example, they'll wonder what you're up to. It's sort of like when you were a teenager living at home. In an office a door that is constantly closed raises a red flag, regardless of whether the person is a clerk or a senior manager.

Maintain a To-Do List

The key to getting things *that count* done is to learn how to set priorities. This may be hard at first, while you're learning what's *really* important and what's *somewhat* important (everything, of course, is important!). The best way to start is to create a to-do list. Begin by jotting down everything you have to do, both your routine tasks and those special jobs your boss assigns to you from time to time. Once you have listed them, give them priorities (1, 2, 3, and so on), based on deadlines you've been given or other indications of urgency (see the next section for more on setting priorities). If you have any doubts, show the list to your boss and ask him or her to verify that you've put things in the right order. Then make a clean list, putting the most important tasks first. Keep this list in a prominent location on your desk or wall. Don't be surprised when you have to keep revising this list as priorities change.

Before you leave work each day, create a *daily* to-do list of the items you must do—and think you can do—the next day. Don't wait until morning to do this—your mind is more in tune with priorities at the end of a workday than it is early in the day, when all looks possible.

This daily list, which is based on your master to-do list, will help focus your efforts. It also gives you goals to shoot for. It will make you very much aware of the time you have available, so you can set mini-deadlines in your mind for that day's work; for example, finish the monthly report before lunch, and work on compiling sales figures until the close of the business day. But the best part of list making is the feeling of accomplishment you get when you cross off the items you've completed.

Some experts recommend doing the hardest tasks early in the day, but it really depends on when you feel you're at your best mentally. It's usually a good idea to save the more mundane jobs for after lunch or just before leaving for the day, when you're likely to be less alert.

Decide What's Most Important

Many, if not most, of the tasks you'll be given in your first year on the job will have deadlines, so that setting priorities will be fairly easy. If someone asks you to so something but doesn't specify a deadline, ask for one. If the person responds with "Oh, whenever you can get to it" or "Sometime this month," then suggest a deadline of your own. "How about two weeks from today—the twelfth?" Make sure, of course, that it's a deadline you can easily make. There's another reason you should always talk dates when talking deadlines: Some people will say, "Whenever you can get to it," but they really mean, "Whenever you can get to it *this week.*" You may not know that until it's too late.

If two or more items have the same deadline, or a huge project's deadline will affect your ability to meet smaller deadlines, you have two choices. The obvious one, and the one you should follow for the first few months on the job, is to check with your boss. You might want to list all of your assignments and their deadlines and show the list to her; this approach is good if you have several priorities that need rearranging. If only one or two deadlines are in contention, just a brief conversation or E-mail message will be sufficient. The second approach is to do the most important tasks first, but this assumes you have the ability to judge priorities correctly.

If you pay attention and ask questions when your boss rearranges priorities for you, you'll begin to get a sense of what's important and what's not as important. You'll probably notice that your boss places priority on tasks that will bring in money— such as doing work that a customer pays for versus administrative tasks that the company's overhead pays for. Once you begin to understand how your boss thinks, you should be able to resolve some of these conflicts on your own.

Setting priorities involves looking at the big picture and deciding what counts the most. To a businessperson, profit may be most important (the business must survive and grow, after all), and profit is tied to other factors, such as sales volume, expenses, and productivity. A company president who has to make a decision among several options will look at each option's likely impact on the bottom line—profit. Of course, profit is not always the most important factor. A company may spend millions of dollars to correct something that would damage its reputation, as when a car manufacturer recalls and repairs, at its cost, a model with safety defects. Or it may have to spend time and money to respond to a government investigation. Sometimes simply staying in business becomes the bottom line.

As you learn more about your job and are expected to make some of your own decisions, you will want to look at each choice you make with an eye toward the bigger picture. If you're not sure what's most important, ask yourself what would happen if each option was delayed or not done. Would your department, division, or company suffer financial losses? Would you get in trouble with customers? Would you get in trouble with your boss? A task's importance becomes fairly clear once you start asking questions like these.

Some tasks seem important but aren't. Let's say your boss asks you to rearrange the departmental library, throw out dated reference materials, and enter all the books into a computer program. It's a big job, and it's all you can think of. In fact, you may not have heard your boss say that you should work on the project during your slow periods. But it takes over in your mind as the biggest job you have, and before you know it, you're well into the task. You submit your weekly report a day late, and there are a stack of phone messages piling up on your desk. If you don't stop to think about priorities soon, your boss will have to come back to remind you.

Another way to set priorities is to compare them against your goals for the year. At some point in your first year, your boss will probably sit down with you to review your progress and establish a few goals for you to complete by the next review date. We'll talk more about this in Chapter 8, but for now let's assume that one of those goals was to write a procedures manual for your job. If you find yourself having to decide which item on your to-do list comes next—work on the library project or start writing the procedures manual—you'd probably be wise to choose the manual. Managers are often quite serious about accomplishing stated goals, and your chances for a raise or a promotion could depend on their completion by the stated time.

Tools You Can Use

A Spiral-Bound Notebook. This type of notebook can be the next best tool you have after your daily calendar. The 6-by-9½-inch size is the easiest to carry. This is important because you'll want to take the notebook everywhere with you—to meetings, to training sessions, to your boss's office. Here's where you'll record phone conversations, instructions, decisions, under-standings, reminders, and so on. Just pretend you're still in school and take notes on everything. Later you'll have a better idea of what to record and what not to, but for now you can't go wrong in jotting all the details down. The benefits are many:

- You won't have to return to your boss quite so often to ask him or her to repeat instructions.
- You'll have a written record of a promise you made—or one that was made to you.
- You'll be able to remember the names of people you spoke to on the phone, the time and date of the call, and the subject of the conversation.
- You'll be able to reconstruct, even months later, what was decided or discussed at a meeting.
- You'll have, at hand, instructions for using any machines or software you were given lessons on.

- If someone has to fill in for you while you're out sick or on vacation, your notebook will serve as a resource of names and tasks.
- You'll have everything in one place, not on backs of envelopes and Post-its scattered all over your desk.

The advantage of a spiral-bound notebook is that everything is recorded in chronological order—just start a new page each day (be sure to write the date at the top of the page). If you need to refresh your memory on how to send word processing files over the E-mail system, you can flip back in your notebook to find the notes from your training session of two weeks ago. It's tempting to use tabbed sections to record information by subject area, but most people end up using the notebook more like a daily journal—it's just easier to find things.

Christina spends a lot of time on the phone with clients and keeps a separate phone journal. She suggests, "Write down notes of every phone conversation, and be sure to note the time and date of the call. This lets you have something concrete to refer to if problems arise later. People often forget what they said over the phone. Also keep a running list of calls you've made and messages you've left, including dates and times."

Your Computer. You probably know how to use Microsoft Word or WordPerfect word processing programs, and perhaps you also know one or two spreadsheet, graphics, or page layout programs as well. What may surprise you is how much you *don't* know about any of the programs you use. In Microsoft Word, for example, did you know you can design pages with newspaper-style columns, maintain mailing lists and create personalized form letters, print labels and envelopes complete with postal service bar codes, and automatically create professional-looking tables and graphs? If you take the time to learn advanced features, you'll be much more efficient and impress your boss at the same time. (She may even ask you for lessons!)

> Jeremy offers this time-saver: "My job in the Marketing Department involves sending information to some of the same people every week. Instead of writing out or typing up mailing labels each time, I've printed out sheets of labels for each addressee. Now all I do is slap on the preprinted labels and the packets are ready to go."

Even if you use only the basic features of one of the popular word processing programs, look into some of the keyboard shortcuts available for common tasks like setting boldface or italic type, saving files, selecting text, and other functions you normally perform with the mouse. You'll be surprised how much quicker it is, for example, to set a word or phrase in italics by pressing the "Control" and "I" keys than by using the mouse to move the cursor to the "I" button on the toolbar in Word. Most computer stores and bookstores carry inexpensive pocket guides that list shortcuts for many popular programs; check your user's manual and on-line help screens as well.

You'll want to be open to learning new programs as you see the need for them. Luckily, most young people take this as a fact of life, not as the challenge and chore that many people over forty view it. If you're given a task to complete that you think might lend itself to being put on a computer, check with your company's computer services group (often called MIS or information systems) to see if the staff can recommend a suitable software package. Say your job is to conduct a two-thousand-person survey. Instead of doing everything manually, you could use a simple program like SurveyPro to design the questionnaire and enter the responses. The software tabulates every-thing and produces the report, much more quickly and accu-rately than you could do manually. Many specialized programs are available for performing rote tasks; you just have to be will-ing to look for them and learn how to use them.

An Address Book or Rolodex. Record phone and fax numbers as well as mailing and E-mail addresses of every person you think you'll need to contact again. If you're not sure, record the infor-mation anyway—you'll never know when it could come in handy. Don't leave this information on phone message slips or scraps of paper that can get lost. Transfer it right away—say, as you're returning a call or mailing a letter—to a Rolodex card or an address book. You may prefer to use the handheld computer devices made for this purpose; just be sure you can keep and update the same information on your computer in case you ever lose the device. Also keep a list of essential office and customer phone numbers at home or in your wallet, in case you need to make calls while you're away from the office.

Checklists. Checklists are a surefire way to be certain you've done everything you were supposed to do. As you're learning a task, checklists can be helpful reminders because they take you through a process step by step. You can devise your own check-lists for the tasks you perform. One good way is to translate your notes or instructions for the task into a simple numbered list of steps or reminders. You can create and store the checklist on the computer, then print out a sheet each time you do the task, checking off the steps as you complete them. Later, as these tasks become second nature to you, you can stop using the checklists. You may want to ask your boss to take a look at any checklists you create to make sure you've included everything and have the steps in the right order.

Using the Telephone and Fax to Your Advantage. The phone and fax are great tools for getting the job done, but they can also waste time if used inefficiently. We covered some of the basics of phone and voice mail etiquette in Chapter 1, so here we'll talk about making the most of your phone. First, keep your calls short and to the point. You can be friendly without being long-winded. If the person you're talking with is too chatty, do what you can to close the conversation, especially if the discussion has moved away from the matter at hand.

Second, learn how to leave good messages, either with a secretary or on voice mail. Give your full name and company name, your phone number, the time you called, and the nature of your call. Also give a time that you can probably be reached at your desk. If you'll be out of the office for the rest of the day, say so. You can leave a more detailed message on voice mail. If all you need from the person is a fact or figure, say so and suggest that the information be left on your voice mail (or sent to you by fax—be sure to give your fax number) if you're not available. This technique will cut down on back-and-forth phone calls that never accomplish anything.

When responding to messages (and we'll assume you'll respond within a day's time whenever possible), you can use the fax and voice mail to answer simple requests for information. If you call before or after the caller's normal working hours or during lunchtime (and be sure to consider the different time zones), you'll be able to leave the information without getting tied up in a conversation, freeing up your time and the other person's. Not all calls lend themselves to this treatment, though—most of the time you'll probably need to talk with the person. If you fail to reach that person on your return call, state in your message a good time to reach you.

If you're waiting for an especially important call, or the telephone tag routine has become an exercise in frustration, ask your receptionist (or whoever answers the incoming calls) to page you over the office intercom when the person in question calls. Be sure this procedure is acceptable office practice before you make the request.

Faxes and E-mail messages are a great way to communicate

lengthy or complex information that would be hard to convey over the phone. If necessary, the person can call you back after he or she has had a chance to see things in writing. If the person is in another city and time is of the essence, you might want to use overnight mail for documents longer than ten or twelve pages—just try to determine when the cost of faxing long distance outweighs the cost of overnight mail (ask your mailroom supervisor or office manager for estimates).

Books, Magazines, and Newsletters. Become familiar with the reference books and periodicals that are read by the professionals in your field. Even though much of their content may not make sense to you yet, you should at least know the kind of information that is available in them for future reference. If your company has a corporate library, spend part of your lunch hour there one day, taking notes and asking questions of the librarian. If there's no library, ask your boss to show you the periodicals and books he or she relies on for news and information about the field.

DEALING WITH PROCRASTINATION

One of the last statements your boss wants to hear you say is "I haven't gotten around to that yet." The reasons for delaying a task are many—the task is difficult or boring, it's more exciting to work under pressure at the last possible minute, or there's a possibility of failing. The hope is that something will intervene and the need to do the dreaded task will go away.

If the task you're postponing is simply tedious and boring, then make yourself set a time (soon) to get it done. Doing the task immediately is best, before something else comes up. Don't let anything else tempt you away, like the need to clean out your files or to make a phone call. This is self-discipline at its toughest. You may have to force yourself to sit at your desk (or wherever you need to be) until you finish. Don't let yourself get up until you're through, or at the point you promised yourself you'd get to. Even if you have to stare at the wall for thirty minutes before you finally get started, do it. After you've completed the task, you'll feel much better, and you may even wonder why you waited so long. Sometimes the thought of getting something done is worse than the actual doing.

If the project is so huge that you don't know where to start, try making a list of all the component tasks, even the smallest ones. Then do a small step or two. That may be enough to give you the momentum and confidence you need to get the rest of the job done.

One executive who was plagued by procrastination came up with a method that worked for her—she made herself do absolutely nothing for fifteen minutes. Once the time was up, she was ready to do anything just to feel that she was moving forward again. Try this if nothing else seems to work (and hope your boss doesn't drop by to see you!).

In her wonderful book for aspiring writers, *Bird by Bird,* Anne Lamott explains the story behind its title: ". . . my brother, who was ten at the time, was trying to get a report on birds written that he'd had three months to write, which was due the next day. . . . He was at the kitchen table close to tears, surrounded by binder paper and pencils and unopened books on birds, immobilized by the hugeness of the task ahead. Then my father sat down beside him, put his arm around my brother's shoulder, and said, 'Bird by bird, buddy. Just take it bird by bird.' "

GETTING THE JOB DONE

One day your boss will ask you to do something that will take several days or even weeks to complete. You'll be in charge, which means you'll have to plan how you will get the job done, get the cooperation of others, and obtain the resources or supplies you'll need. If you've been used to completing small, fairly simple tasks to this point, you could be daunted by this challenge. But if you can keep in mind that all big jobs are actually just many small jobs combined, you can avoid having the project overwhelm you. Just take things one step at a time.

Clarify Instructions and Expectations

First, make absolutely sure you know what you're being asked to do. Take notes as your boss describes the project to you. Ask questions about anything you don't understand. Find out exactly what you're supposed to deliver—is it a written report, an oral presentation, or just a handwritten note to let your boss know you've completed the job? When you get back to your desk, review your notes. You'll almost certainly have two or three more questions. Get them answered as soon as you can.

Anytime you find yourself saying, "Well, I assume my boss means this" or "I imagine it'll take the engineers a day to answer my questions," stop yourself. Assumptions can get you into big trouble. Always make sure that your assumptions are in fact true. It doesn't take long to double-check, and the mistake you prevent could be your own. Assumptions about people's intentions and reasoning can also be wrong. If there's any possibility for misunderstanding—and there usually is—ask specific, concrete questions that will clarify what needs to be done.

Be sure to get a deadline. Push for one if your boss says something like "Whenever." This is for your own protection, because deep down he has a deadline in mind, and his idea of "whenever" is surely going to be earlier than yours. You will want to mark the final due date and any interim due dates your boss may have mentioned on a calendar when you create your schedule. Work backward from the final due date, allotting time for the separate steps involved.

Find out what resources—people, files, programs—your boss would recommend using to complete the job. Without being too obnoxious, pick his brain until you think he's given you all he can on the subject. You won't be embarrassing yourself or showing your ignorance—it's just that all of those details are second nature to him, and it won't occur to him to share them unless you ask.

Get the Help You Need

You'll find that no matter how large or small the project, you'll be relying on other people to help you get your job done. Whether they are inside or outside your company, the people you'll be working with will be expecting you to—

- Treat them with courtesy and respect, regardless of their title, so don't put your requests in the form of a command. And don't forget that your tone of voice is just as important as the words you use.
- Consider the many other demands on their time—you're not the only person they're working with.
- Give them a clear idea of what you need and sufficient time in which to get it done.
- Ask what you can do to make the task easier for them.
- Show appreciation for what they've done for you, even if it's a basic part of their job.
- Be ready to return the favor when they need help, ideally as soon as you can.

Because of your entry-level status in the company, you may find it harder to enlist the help of others at first. For one thing, they may believe that you won't ever be able to repay their help (of course, you could be their boss someday, and some sharp people will realize that). For another, they'd rather spend their time helping someone with more visibility or someone they already know and like. For these reasons, it's especially important to be friendly, low-key, and considerate when making your requests. Most people, especially in support positions, are so used to being ordered around that a little kindness and consideration will go a long way in gaining their cooperation.

You may have to go around someone who's become a real barrier. Talk with your boss about the problem and discuss alternatives. Don't ignore the situation. If it's clear that a particular coworker is not interested in cooperating, don't expect that this person might have a change of heart before your deadline comes. It's also not a good idea to wait until the end and then tell your boss, "Well, Jan would never return my calls, so I couldn't finish that part." It's your responsibility to see that the job gets done; any excuses will have to be spectacular ones.

Be Flexible

Don't be surprised when something comes up that upsets your well-made plans. In fact, *expect* that things will change—your boss will toss in a new requirement at the last minute, the customer will change specifications, your most important source of help will get transferred to another part of the company—the possibilities are endless. One of the most useful attitudes you can develop is flexibility. Don't panic; just stay calm and take a few minutes to think about the implications of the change and alternative ways of handling the situation. Confer with your boss if you need to. But don't waste your time and energy getting angry or upset—doing so won't change anything, and you'll be seen as more professional if you simply carry on the best you can.

If You'll Be Working on a Team Effort

It's likely that you'll be assigned to work as a member of a team at some point in your first year. Again, because you will be new to the group, you can expect to get the least exciting work. But don't grumble and gripe about it—you're being watched and tested by your colleagues, who want to see how well you'll fit in. If you're confident (not cocky), open, agreeable, and ready to do just about anything, they'll be more likely to want you on their team in the future. If you participate during team meetings and contribute a good idea once in a while, you'll be considered a full-fledged member in no time.

Sharing Information and Ideas. Sharing information and ideas will ensure your acceptance as a team member. Don't just sit silently through every meeting—participate, showing your interest and willingness to work, with one warning: Make sure you have something of value to offer. Don't talk just for the sake of talking, or to impress others with your knowledge. People will see right through you. Also, take a positive, not an aggressive, tone. You want to become part of the team, not remain an outsider.

Since you'll be viewed as the new kid and won't be given much weight at first—in fact, you may even be seen as a threat by some—you may want to piggyback your ideas onto those of one of the other team members. For example, let's say you have an idea to start an information hot line for your company's services. In the marketing committee meeting, you look for an appropriate time to piggyback your idea onto someone else's: "If we go ahead with Joe's idea to create a new marketing brochure, that might be a good time to start offering a telephone hot line that would let people call for more information. We could print the number on the brochure." This approach often works because it seems as if you've merely enhanced someone else's idea, which people are more likely to accept. In addition, your support for your colleague's idea may cause him to return the favor and support yours. (See more about selling your ideas in the next chapter.)

If you have an idea you'd like to propose, be sure to think it through before presenting it. Anticipate any objections or arguments so that you can counter them in a professional way.

Getting Along with Difficult People. You'll inevitably have to work with people you disagree with or don't get along with. You'll have to learn to voice your disagreements in the most inoffensive way possible. "I think the plan to phone one thousand customers by Friday may be overoptimistic" is more tactful than "Ann, that's a stupid idea. How could we ever reach that many people in such a short time!" If your objection is overruled, you'll still need to do your part as graciously as you can. Offering solutions or compromises is a more constructive way to disagree. For example, you might say something like "I think Ann's idea to conduct a customer survey is a good one. Perhaps we could hire some local business school students part-time to help us get it completed more quickly."

Remember, in every office there are people who are abrasive, unpleasant, rude, or self-centered. But you must be able to work with such people. Here, the important thing is to accomplish the team goal, not to get along like old college friends. In earlier chapters, we talked about the need to accept people for who they are. You'll never be able to change people—think how hard it is to change some aspect of your own behavior—so don't waste your time trying or complaining about the situation.

Don't be surprised—or upset—if people say negative things to you or ignore your ideas and comments. You can make yourself miserable by taking these things too seriously. In fact, one of the best traits you can work on developing is a thick skin. If you are too sensitive, you'll tend to play it safe in order to avoid negative reactions, and eventually you'll be left behind. Most successful managers say that their refusal to let negative remarks get them down was crucial to getting ahead.

Knowing the Importance of Follow-Through. Following through—on questions to be answered, tasks to be done, calls to be made—is more important than ever when you're involved in a team effort. If you drop the ball, you could be affecting the progress of the team as a whole. Worse still, everyone will know it. Make sure that when you leave team meetings, the assignments are clearly defined. If you're not sure, double-check by asking the team leader something like "Now, you'd like me to check on the status of the new product with the Engineering Group and let everyone know by Tuesday, right?" As stressed earlier in this chapter, don't trust details to your memory—write everything down on your to-do list. Up to now, perhaps only your boss knew your strengths and weaknesses; on a team, many people will be depending on you and seeing firsthand how you operate. Your future progress in the company could depend a lot on how well you perform as a team member.

Learn to Juggle Priorities

Sooner or later you'll find yourself facing two or three tasks that need to be done at the same time. Your first instinct may be to panic ("How can I possibly get all this done by Wednesday!"), perhaps to the point of near shutdown ("Why even try? It's impossible. Something has to give"). Assuming that your problem was not caused by your own procrastination, there's usually a way to get everything done.

The first step is to take a few minutes to look objectively at the requirements of each task. Take Task 1 and break it into parts that you can assign time estimates to; be realistic, not optimistic, when you judge the time required. Often you'll find that the total time needed is less than you imagined. (Fear has a way of magnifying things.) Do the same for the other tasks that are vying for your time, and then plot those times out on your calendar. You may find that things aren't so impossible after all. But if they are, ask your boss to help you sort things out. Show her your time estimates (she'll be impressed that you've taken such a professional approach and have tried to solve the problem on your own). You might ask if you could have an extension on one of the tasks, or if she has any advice on how you could complete a task more efficiently.

If you think your boss won't want to hear about your problem, then you may have no choice but to stay late or take work home with you to do on your own time. At first you may need to do this while you're learning the ropes—most things take longer the first few times you do them. As you settle in to the job, you'll find you'll get better at arranging priorities and doing tasks more efficiently. Don't feel bad; this happens to everybody during their first few months on the job—any job.

One of the time-honored principles of business life is the "unattainable triad." Picture a triangle with one side labeled "cost," another labeled "time," and the third labeled "quality." The rule is that you can have two out of the three elements: You can have it right away and at low cost, but the quality will suffer; you can have it perfect and on time, but it will cost more; or you can have it perfect and for a reasonable price, but it will take more time. Satisfying all three demands is impossible because they conflict. Sometimes it's helpful to use this principle to determine what's most important.

Know When to Say No

You probably don't feel that you can say no to a request when you're so new to the job, and in many cases this will be true. But if you're good at what you do, you'll soon find that people will be asking you for more and more. At some point—and this is a judgment call—you'll have to say no, or "not right now." You can quickly explain the reasons, but don't spend twenty minutes going into detail about every task you're doing—nobody will really care once you've stated that you can't be of help. You can soften the blow by asking if the task can be done at a later time.

It's not a good idea to turn down your boss or anyone else in a higher-level position. When these requests come, you'll need to reshuffle priorities, perhaps with your boss's help.

Be careful about overcommitting yourself to too many things; the minute you can't get everything done, you'll earn a reputation for being unreliable. The same goes for promising to have a task done by a certain date. It may be tempting to say you'll have it done by Thursday, but you may want to qualify your promise with words like "if all goes well." Or you may simply say, "I'll do my best to have it done by Thursday, and I'll let you know by Wednesday if there'll be a problem." Or you may think you can have it done by Thursday, but you promise it by Friday, just to give yourself extra time in case unexpected events cause delays. If you can deliver "early" on Thursday, you'll look good.

Keep Your Boss Informed

Managers vary in their need to be kept informed. Some want to know what you've done each day, while others will seem barely interested in your activities. Most are somewhere in between. If your boss doesn't make it clear how she'd like to be updated on your work, ask her how often and in what form—written report, E-mail message, informal office visit—she'd like to hear from you. But don't let it go at that.

She may say a weekly summary is fine. But if you're working on a project that is especially important to her, you may find that she drops in daily to see how things are going. Take the hint and start keeping her informed more frequently. In short, try to figure out where her comfort level is and communicate with her at that level.

Turn in Quality Work

It's tempting, when you're feeling rushed and overwhelmed, to rush through tasks as quickly as you can. In your desire to get started, you may think it would take too much time to sit down and map out a plan of attack. Instead, you jump right in so you can feel that you're moving ahead, only to realize later that you forgot to arrange for a key item and must start over. There's a proverb that advises, "To finish sooner, take your time." The same advice applies to doing quality work. A few hours spent in thinking things through and mapping out a plan almost always pay off, even if things change down the road. Once you're deep into the work, take it at a calm and steady pace, not a hectic, rushed one. When your mind is in panic mode, it can't think clearly, and you will miss things that will be hard or even impossible to correct later.

Take the time to save your work frequently on your computer—as often as every fifteen minutes or so. You can set your computer to do this automatically. Make backup copies on disk at the end of each work session. You may never need them, but if your system fails, as it surely will someday, you'll never regret the time it took to make the copies.

Avoid turning in work that has errors—typos, arithmetic mistakes, or inaccurate information. If something has numerous errors, people will focus on the deficiencies rather than on the overall job, and all your hard work will be overlooked. You don't want to get a reputation for being sloppy or inept this early in your career. Don't rely totally on your computer's spell-checker. Take the time to read everything through once or twice. Ask a coworker to check behind you, and offer to return the favor. Double-check any math as well as phone numbers, addresses, and the spelling of proper names. The time you spend doing this will help ensure your reputation as a competent, professional employee.

HOW TO HANDLE FAILURE

Don't expect that you'll be able to do every job handed to you perfectly. As hard as you'll try, some things just won't work out as planned. Accept this as a fact of life so that you won't be devastated when failure happens.

Many people are so afraid to fail that they never try anything new. This attitude will limit your progress and make you unhappy in the long run. If you read about successful people, you'll see that almost all of them experienced episodes of failure throughout their lives but that they refused to let it get them down for very long.

There is an old saying that we learn from our failures, not our successes. Think about it. You may have always wanted to be a computer programmer, but you can't seem to write code without a great deal of difficulty. You finally decide to admit defeat in that field, but find that you can combine your language skills with your technical knowledge, and you start to build a career as a technical writer. Or you may have made a major error in judgment that meant a late delivery on a project; your boss was upset but forgave you, and you know you'll never make the same kind of mistake again.

Don't hesitate to take on a difficult task because you're afraid you'll fail. The truth is, you'll never know what you can accomplish unless you try. If you fail, so what? You're that much smarter than when you began. If you never take risks, you'll never fail, but you'll never get ahead, either.

If you do fail, don't let it get you down for long. The best you can do is figure out what you can learn from the experience and then put it behind you. Don't dwell on it, and don't let it permanently mark you. You're human, and failure happens.

7

Communicating Clearly

If you can speak and write so that your meaning is clear and easily understood, you'll be miles ahead of most people in the business world. No special talent is required, but you do need to know about a few common pitfalls. This chapter will cover the three types of business communication: person-to-person; written memos, letters, and reports; and oral presentations.

COMMUNICATING ON A PERSONAL LEVEL

Speaking So That You Won't Be Misunderstood

Probably the biggest challenge in human communication is to speak so that you are not *misunderstood*. Once you go beyond the niceties of everyday conversation ("How are things going?" "What did you do this weekend?" and so on), you'll run into two major problems: People don't listen well, and people hear what they want, or expect, to hear.

How many times have you found yourself drifting off into your own thoughts while someone was talking to you? We all do it—our brains work so fast that they can listen to someone and still have room to process a variety of internal thoughts. The problem is that even though the brain can do this, it doesn't do it very well. If we're not concentrating on what the speaker is saying, our own thoughts are going to block out the speaker's. (See "Learning to Listen" in Chapter 3.) We also often make the mistake of hearing what we *expect* to hear. When you're talking, how can you be sure the person you're speaking to hears exactly what you want to communicate?

One way is to try speaking slowly and deliberately, without being condescending. This doesn't guarantee that the listener will focus on you, but it sometimes seems to work better than talking quickly and randomly. But don't speak too slowly. Periodic pauses might work well to attract audience attention in public speaking, but they're dangerous on a personal level because they seem to invite the other person to jump in. If you find that you're frequently interrupted when you're trying to explain something, ask your listener to give you a chance to finish—you can do this so nicely that it doesn't come across as a rebuke.

Jessica says, "My boss talks fast. When he's giving me a list of things to do, I have to ask him to slow down. He doesn't realize he's doing it. Don't be afraid to ask someone to slow down or repeat something—it's better to know for sure than to fail to get all the information you need."

You can make sure you've been understood by asking the listener questions about what you just said. Unfortunately, this technique may be off-limits to you because of your lower-level position—such questions are more appropriate coming from a superior. But there are ways around this situation. When you're through, you might say something like "So, to summarize, here's what I'd like to do . . ." or "To wrap up, here's how I propose that this works . . . Is that okay with you?" Find a way to repeat your important points to be sure you were completely heard—it will save you a lot of grief later.

There will be times when you know that the person you're talking with isn't hearing (that is, understanding) a word you say. You can tell that your coworker's brain is working on what to say next rather than listening to you. This is extremely frustrating, and there's not much you can do about it. Just be aware that the person has not really heard you, and try to repeat the most important information. Think about television commercials. One of the basic principles of advertising is repetition—of the message (perhaps five times in one hour) and the name brand and product image. Poor listening and retention is human nature, so you must learn to work around it.

At times it's a good idea to put your points in writing. Prepare a brief memo, stating the most important items of the discussion (things like deadlines, expectations, desired results, and so on). Handing the memo to the person or persons either before or after your conversation will ensure that you won't be misunderstood. You can downplay the formality by saying something like "I wrote these things down so they'd be easy for us to refer to later" or "I don't want to waste your time, and I find that putting things on paper helps me organize my thoughts."

Interpreting Different Speaking Styles

When it comes to speaking, experts say that there are two types of people: those who are more abstract and emotional, preferring to speak in general terms and to look at things flexibly; and those who are more objective and logical, preferring details and order. If you can figure out the type of person you're talking to, you can improve your chances of being understood by speaking accordingly. For example, the ordered and logical person will love it if you say something like "With your help, here are the three things I'd like to do by Tuesday. . . ." The same statement might make a more flexible person uncomfortable—your coworker may think you're being too rigid and unrealistic. After all, other events could happen between now and Tuesday that would throw off your careful plans. To this person you might say,

"With your help, I'd like to accomplish a few things by next week if possible."

Some people, perhaps to be courteous or to show respect, word their requests so vaguely that people misunderstand them. If your boss says to you, "Perhaps we should think about getting this done soon," you may be thinking "low priority," while she really means, "If you don't have this done by Friday, you're in trouble." Be sure to question any vague requests to get down to the details—pin the person down to dates, times, specific instructions.

A frequently heard phrase is "Are you busy?" It really means, "I have something I need you to do." If a superior says this to you, your answer should be "Not too busy to help—what can I do for you?" Here's the all-time classic: "When you have a minute, I'd like to speak with you." This really means, "I'd like to speak with you right now."

> Jeb deals with his boss's verbal style like this: "My boss doesn't make a lot of demands of me, but sometimes he'll say, 'If you have some extra time . . . ' and then he finishes by say-ing, 'I know it'll probably take you awhile.' I always try to get these tasks done as soon as possible. Bosses like that."

Finally, don't be surprised if your boss asks for your opinion or ideas on something, then seems to ignore your input. There could be several reasons: He wants to seem democratic; he mis-takenly thinks he's "empowering" you, a popular management theory these days; he forgot or didn't understand what you said; or he didn't like what you said. Of course, he could love your idea and is waiting for the right time to use it.

Selling Your Ideas

After you've been on the job for a few months, you'll probably have some ideas on how to streamline a process or do something in a new way. That's great—you're thinking and showing initiative, which is important to your success. Many of the ideas you'll have early on will be specific to your job, and your boss will probably encourage you to go ahead with them. As you learn more about the company, you'll probably have bigger ideas, the kind that will make an impact (and perhaps get you some recognition). Many young people get discouraged, however, because it's so hard to convince people to adopt new ways. But you can improve your chances by taking three important steps:

• Make sure your idea hasn't been tried (and failed) in the past few years. If it has, do some research and troubleshoot earlier mistakes before proposing it again—with fixes.
• Think out the idea from all angles, and make sure that what you're proposing will save money, not cost money.
• Take into account everyone who will be affected if your idea is implemented.

The first step is easy—ask the people around you. The second step takes a little more research, but it will be crucial to documenting your claims. Can you quantify how much time or money your idea will save? If your idea will cost the company more money, you may as well forget it, unless you can convince your boss that such an expense will result in increased revenues down the road.

The third step may be the most important of all. You should recognize that most people don't like change, good or bad. If you can involve the people who will be affected by your idea, and get them to contribute their own thoughts and suggestions (and then you'll need to make sure you consider them), you'll have a fighting chance. You should also realize that people other than your boss may have to approve a change in methods or procedures. Will your boss have to convince his boss, or will Human Resources (or Accounting or Computer Services) have to give its approval?

When you've considered every angle and gathered every cost estimate you can think of, stop and try to anticipate the opposition. Tear your idea apart, thinking of all the possible objections to it. After you've done this, you're ready to present your idea to your boss—in person if possible, so you can answer questions as they arise. But be sure to consider the timing of your request. Try not to bring up your plan when your boss is in a bad mood or bogged down in some major crisis. If your idea will cost money, hold off until you're sure the department or company is not in a financial pinch.

Being the Kind of Person People Like to Talk To (and Work With)

The biggest part of good "people skills" is good communication skills. Are you a good listener? Do you limit your complaints, but patiently listen to the problems and complaints of others (for a while, at least)? Are you empathetic—that is, do you try to understand the concerns and feelings of others, putting yourself in their shoes? Do you let people talk without frequent interruptions? Do you let others do most of the talking, or do you hog the conversation? Do you keep harsh criticisms of others to yourself, or are you judgmental and opinionated? Are you pleasant and enthusiastic, or are you grouchy much of the time?

If you are comfortable with small talk—the day-to-day conversations about sports, the weather, family, clothes, travel, and so on—you'll be perceived as someone who is friendly, open, and approachable. This will make it easier for you to be heard and believed when serious conversations take place. If you think you are above small talk or not good at it, consider the implications. You may risk coming across as an arrogant, "too good for us" type of person, and that will hurt you later. It's not that hard to engage in everyday, informal chitchat, even if you're painfully shy. But it will be difficult for you to move ahead if people feel they can't relate to you on a personal as well as on a business level.

Felicia, an account executive for a printing company, says, "My boss has to deal with a lot of different types of customers in various businesses. To relate to them, he keeps up with happenings in a lot of different areas, including the stock market, auto racing, music, and banking. Needless to say, his interest in his customers' fields makes him easy to get along with, which doesn't hurt when it comes to closing business deals."

Dealing with Disagreements

Chapter 4 talked about getting along with difficult people, and explained that it's unlikely you'll always agree with everyone. If you can keep that thought in mind, it will be easier for you not to feel hurt, threatened, or angry when disagreements arise, as they will.

When you find yourself disagreeing with someone, try to keep your cool at all costs. The minute you explode, you'll have marked yourself, perhaps for life. The word will spread like wildfire throughout the office that you have a short fuse. People will avoid you, and your boss will be hesitant to promote you. This is not an exaggeration. If a situation becomes intolerable or you feel you're losing control, excuse yourself and leave the room. Go outside, or to the rest room, until you cool down.

When you feel you can be rational, resume your conversation, and calmly make your thoughts known. Listen attentively to the other person. You may have to end your discussion by agreeing to disagree. There doesn't always have to be a winner; what matters is that you must still be able to work together.

If your disagreement is with a customer, be very careful what you say. This is not the time to get into an argument. It's best to suggest resuming the conversation after you've had a chance to discuss the problem with your boss. This approach also has the advantage of letting your boss know that you're handling the situation appropriately. If difficulties with the person continue, it may be best to turn the account over to someone else in your department. Try not to take such a transfer personally; there will be some people that you will not be able to relate well to, no matter how hard you try.

What about when people openly attack you, or do so behind your back? You have two choices: You can either confront the attacker (make sure you have enough evidence to do so), or you can ignore the situation. It's probably best to go to the person and state what you've heard, and ask for an explanation. Your gutsiness will often be enough to stop any future attacks.

Writing the Easy Way

Many businesspeople think that letters, memos, and reports must be written in a formal way, using lots of professional-sounding terms and phrases. Young people entering government service, for example, think they must master a certain bureaucratic writing style if they're to be taken seriously. Don't make these mistakes. The worst thing you can do is try to copy the style of the bad writing you see around you. If you have to read something twice to understand it, then it's not written well.

The secret of good business writing is to write the way you talk. This advice assumes, of course, that you don't ramble on and that you can get to the point quickly and clearly. When you sit down to write a letter or a memo or even a report, think what you'd say if the person you're writing to were sitting across from you. You wouldn't say, "Due to the inability of the manufacturer to effect conveyance of the requisite parts to our distributor in a timely fashion, we must regretfully inform you that our work on your equipment will be protracted." No, you'd probably say something like "We won't be able to repair your machine as scheduled because we haven't received the parts from the manufacturer yet."

Other than to clean up some of the slang and relaxed grammar that might be acceptable in everyday speech, all you have to do is write as simply as you speak. Don't feel you must dress up your writing with long, complex sentences and fancy words. Keep things short, simple, and to the point.

Here's a good exercise for learning how to get to the point quickly and clearly: Imagine you are in an elevator with the person you're writing your letter or report to, and you have from the twelfth floor to the first floor to state what you want the person to know. What would you say? If you try this mental trick when you sit down to write, you'll find it will help focus your thoughts on the most important points. Those will become your first sentences and paragraphs.

To write clearly, you must think clearly. You have to know what you want to say before you even start to write. Here are some tips to help you organize your thoughts:

• Before you touch the computer keyboard, think about what you need to say. Write down a word or a phrase to remind you of each major item. Then think about which item is most important, which is the next most important, and so on. Put numbers next to each item to show its order of importance. Believe it or not, you've just created an outline.

• Now go to your keyboard and start to write, as if you were talking directly to someone, about item number 1. Then proceed, in order, to the other items on your list, making each one a new paragraph.

• When you've written up all the items on your list, read the entire piece through, adding words and phrases to tie things together as you need them. You may want to add an introductory paragraph explaining the reason for your letter or report, and you may want to put a summary and closing statements at the end. If the document is more than a page or two, you may even want to add headings above each main topic, to help the reader find things. All of these steps are easy because you've already written the hard part. (Keep in mind that a good, "to the point" business letter rarely needs to be more than one page long.)

• Read your document carefully one more time to make sure you haven't forgotten to say something. Journalism students are taught to include the five *W*'s and the *H*—who, what, when, where, why, and how—in each news story; you may want to follow that advice to be sure you've covered everything. Also look for sentences that are too long. Fix them by cutting out unnecessary words or splitting them into two sentences. Then run the spell-checker.

• Print out the document and ask your boss or a coworker to read it. (Offer to return the favor.) That person will probably find a few typos the spell-checker missed, and perhaps a few sentences that need editing. Don't be concerned—even the best writers rarely create perfect first drafts.

• Make your final revisions and run the spell-checker one more time—it's amazing how many typos can creep in on that last round. Then read the document word for word one more time after it's printed out.

The process just described is usually sufficient for the basic kinds of writing you'll do at work. If you ever have to write something that will be read by several other people or published in some way, you'll want to make sure that your writing is the best it can be. The reason for this is that people will judge you by how you write. If your document is full of errors, your readers will assume that you're sloppy, careless, not too bright, or all three. The next section explains how to edit your own work to save yourself from embarrassment.

Editing Your Own Writing

The first rule for editing your own writing is to set your draft aside for a day, or at least a few hours. If you look at it too soon, the words you've chosen will still be fresh in your mind and will sound okay to you. If you take a break between your writing time and your editing time, you'll be able to review your writing more objectively.

Next, read it for content. Find a time and place where you won't be interrupted, and read a printout all the way through—without a pen or pencil in hand—for content only. When you're through, think about what you said. Did you cover all the points you wanted to make? Did you say anything that the reader doesn't really need to know? Did the organization seem okay, or was something out of order? Now take a pen and mark any paragraphs that need to be moved around or deleted. Also note anything that needs to be added or expanded.

Finally, read the paper again for problems in language. This step is the hardest for people who feel that their command of the rules of English is weak. We'll cover the most common grammar, usage, and punctuation mistakes in the following paragraphs. If you can master these, you'll soon have your coworkers coming to you for advice and help.

Keep Sentences Short. It's good to have a mix of sentence lengths, but try to keep the *average* number of words in a sentence to twenty. Sentences that exceed thirty words are usually hard to read, unless they contain lists.

Use the Active Voice. Here's an example of a sentence written in the active voice: "I wrote this report." Here's the same sentence written in the passive voice: "This report was written by me." A sentence written in the passive voice is longer and often vague as to who or what was responsible for the action mentioned. If you had said, "This report was written yesterday," for example, the listener wouldn't know *who* had written it. For people who don't want to take responsibility or blame, the passive voice is very handy. There are times, however, when the passive voice is acceptable, such as when the "actor" of the situation is unknown or unimportant ("The package was delivered at noon today").

But use the active voice whenever you can—it will keep your sentences shorter and your words stronger.

Use Simple, Concrete Words. Don't try to impress people with long or fancy words. The best writers keep things simple. If you remember that your goal is to get your message across, you'll realize that you should make things as easy as possible for the reader. Substitute *terrible* for *egregious, ask* for *interrogate, explain* for *elucidate.*

Don't Make Nouns Out of Verbs. One of the quickest ways to improve your writing is to search out and destroy phrases like *performed an examination, made a determination, came to the realization,* and countless others that contain the *-tion* ending. In almost every case, you can replace these phrases with a single verb, such as *examined, determined,* and *realized* in the above examples. Make a single pass through your document to look for these phrases—the *-tion* ending will be your clue. You'll be surprised how many you'll find and how easy it is to fix them.

Don't Go Overboard with Prepositional Phrases. You can further shorten and strengthen your writing by replacing wordy prepositional phrases with a single word. Here are just a few examples:

Instead of—	*Use—*
in order to	to
at the present time	now
on account of	because
in the event of	if
for the reason that	because
due to the fact that	because

When you see a clumsy prepositional phrase, see if you can replace it with a single, simple word.

Don't Be Redundant. Redundancy can occur in two ways: You can say the same thing twice in different parts of your document, and you can use phrases that contain two words that mean the same thing. You'll probably catch the first kind of redundancy when you read your document for content (but keep in mind that a little redundancy (repetition) is all right if it reinforces a point or serves as a reminder). Catching redundant words is a little harder because we've grown so accustomed to hearing them. These include phrases like "assembled *together,*" "consensus *of opinion,*" "repeat *again,*" "connect *together,*" "reserve *in advance,*" "close *proximity,*" "*free* gift," "*invited* guest," "*serious* danger," and "*prototype* model." The italicized words are unnecessary. Another common form of redundancy occurs with acronyms, when the word that represents the last letter of the acronym is repeated; for example, *HIV virus, SIC code, CD disc.*

Check for Proper Placement of Words. Make sure that the order of your words doesn't mess up your meaning. For example, *only* is a word that must be placed correctly to ensure that the meaning is correct. "She said that she *only liked* me" (she didn't love me) is not the same as "She said that she liked *only me*" (she didn't like anyone else).

Dangling modifier is the grammatical term for a phrase that seems to modify a word that it can't sensibly modify. Whenever you start a sentence with a phrase like one of the following, check to make sure that the word on the other side of the comma makes sense there: "After serving the guests, the movie started." (The movie didn't serve the guests.) "Upon arriving in New York, her loneliness disappeared." (The woman arrived in New York, not her loneliness.)

Use the Right Word. Many words in English sound similar but have completely different meanings. Other words have similar meanings but differ in important ways. Several of the books listed under Writing References in the Recommended Reading section at the end of this book carry extensive listings of these misused and confused words. You should have one of these books at your desk, along with a recent edition of a college dictionary, like *Webster's Collegiate Dictionary,* tenth edition. Here are a few of the most common confusing word pairs in business writing:

affect	to have an influence on
effect	the result (noun); to cause (verb)
among	a relationship of three or more persons or objects
between	a relationship of two persons or objects
amount	a bulk or aggregate quantity
number	a quantity that is countable
anticipate	to prepare for an event
expect	to think an event will happen
appraise	to evaluate
apprise	to inform
complement	to accompany or enhance something
compliment	to express admiration for
compose	to make up the whole; the whole is *composed* of the parts
comprise	to contain; the whole *comprises* the parts
copyright	legal protection for a written or other artistic work
copywrite	*this is not a word,* although people who write advertising copy are called *copywriters*
cost	the amount paid for a thing
price	the amount a seller asks
council	a deliberating body
counsel	to give advice or guidance; also a noun meaning *advice; lawyer*
discreet	careful, prudent
discrete	disconnected, separate

disinterested	impartial
uninterested	indifferent, not interested
flaunt	to show off
flout	to scorn or ignore
foreword	opening statement in a book
forward	near the front, ahead
it's	contraction of *it is*
its	possessive form of pronoun *it*
lay	to set down (past tense *laid*)
lie	to recline (past tense *lay*)
personal	relating to a person
personnel	workforce
principal	most important; a leading person; the original part of an investment
principle	a basic belief or code of conduct
regrettable	describing a condition that causes or calls for regret
regretful	full of regret
stationary	fixed or immobile
stationery	writing paper
their	possessive form of pronoun *they*
they're	contraction of *they are*
who's	contraction of *who is*
whose	possessive form of pronoun *who*
you're	contraction of *you are*
your	possessive form of pronoun *you*

Common Grammar Goofs. You don't need to go back to freshman English class to learn how to avoid making the five most common errors in grammar. If you can conquer the problems discussed here, you'll be ahead of most people. The first is the misuse of *I* and *me.*

Wrong:	Me and Sue went to the movies.
Right:	*Sue and I* went to the movies.
Wrong:	He called Joe and I to the meeting.
Right:	He called *Joe and me* to the meeting.
Wrong:	Just between you and I . . .
Right:	Just between *you and me* . . .

Most of the problems with *I* or *me* occur in sentences that contain *and.* The quickest way to figure out which pronoun is correct is to mentally drop the proper noun or other pronoun and the word *and* and see which sounds right: "*I* went to the movies" (*not* "Me went to the movies") and "He called *me* to the meeting" (*not* "He called I to the meeting"). You can't go wrong using this trick.

The next problem is the misuse of *myself.* In general, use it only to refer back to yourself, as in the sentence "I fixed the problem myself." In most cases, the word *me* or *I* is correct.

Wrong:	She presented the awards to June and myself.
Right:	She presented the awards to June and *me.*
Wrong:	Michael and myself gave the demonstration
Right:	Michael and I gave the demonstration.

Here's another common pronoun problem.

Wrong:	I spoke with he and Bob yesterday.
Right:	I spoke with *him* and Bob yesterday.

Again, an easy way to catch this problem is to mentally eliminate the *and Bob* phrase from the sentence, and you'll know right away which is right: "I spoke with *him,*" not "I spoke with he."

Subject-verb agreement is another frequent error. The biggest problem occurs when other words and phrases fall between the subject and verb, confusing things.

Wrong: His record of achievements and awards are impressive.

Right: His record of achievements and awards *is* impressive.

The subject of the sentence is *record,* not *achievements and awards.* The verb must agree with the subject of the sentence, which—in sentences like the one above—is usually the word before the prepositional phrase *(of achievements and awards).*

One of the most common errors in English is the use of *badly* when *bad* is correct.

Wrong: I felt badly that she couldn't join us.

Right: I felt *bad* that she couldn't join us.

Always use *bad* with the verbs that refer to one of the five senses, such as *appear, sound, feel, taste, seem, become,* and *smell.* The word *badly* is correct with all other verbs.

Wrong: The team performed bad.

Right: The team performed *badly.*

For help with other grammar problems, refer to one of the books listed under Writing References in the Recommended Reading section at the end of this book.

Make Items in a List Parallel in Form. This simply means that all the phrases or sentences that make up a list should be cast in the same grammatical form. That is, in a list of three items, one item should not start with a verb while the second starts with a gerund (nouns that end in -ing) and the third starts with a pronoun. For example—

Wrong:
The administrative assistant will do the following:

1. Open all correspondence.
2. The filing of office documents.
3. He or she will answer the phone.

Right:
The administrative assistant will—

1. Open all correspondence.
2. File office documents.
3. Answer the phone.

Depending on how you word the phrase or sentence that introduces the list, you could start the list items with verbs, gerunds, or nouns—it really doesn't matter which you choose. What *does* matter is that you treat each list item the same way. Most people find that it's easiest and most effective to start list items with verbs, as we did in the correct example. It's okay to have several different kinds of lists within a document, however. By the way, you should try to keep your use of punctuation at the ends of list items consistent. There's no single correct way, so just decide on an approach that makes sense to you and follow it throughout.

Use Consistent Capitalization, Hyphenation, and Number Style. These are the fine points of written communication. While they're not as important as some of the points we've discussed so far, they do play a part in making a document more professional looking. Editors refer to such matters of consistency as *style points,* and they use style manuals to help them make decisions. Usually there is no right or wrong way—consistency is the only rule.

Examples of style points in business writing include when to capitalize names of departments and titles of people (Joe Smith is our *Vice President* for *Human Resources*—or *vice president* for *human resources?*); when to use hyphens *(a well-run office,* but *the office is well run); and* whether to spell out numbers or use numerals (*10* divisions or *ten* divisions?). Many companies follow one of the several published style manuals so that people can stay consistent and avoid spending time making lots of little decisions. If your company has a corporate communications or publications office, find out which guide the office uses—there may even be a company style guide for employees to follow.

Watch the Tone of Your Writing. Make sure that you don't write in a way that reveals any negative thoughts you may have. Don't let sarcastic or angry thoughts come through. Avoid sounding demanding, preachy, or overbearing. Your writing will be much more effective if it is businesslike, to the point, and friendly in tone. If you find yourself writing something in anger or frustration, wait a day or two before deciding to send it. Ninety-five percent of the time you'll be glad you did.

Some Advice on Communicating with E-mail

E-mail is fast becoming the most common form of business communication. It is often misused, usually to the detriment of the sender. Here are a few tips to remember about E-mail:

• Never send an angry or argumentative message, and never send a message you wouldn't want the entire office to read. This includes criticisms of fellow employees. It's easy for the recipient to print out a message or forward it to other people.

• Limit your use of humor unless you are writing to someone who knows you well. Humor in E-mail can be easily misread.

• Never send an urgent message via E-mail. Some people read messages only once a day.

• Keep your messages short and succinct. If your message is so long that the recipient has to print it out to read it easily, it's too long.

• Don't share personal problems with anyone, even your boss, over E-mail. E-mail printouts have been known to sit at shared printers for everyone to read. If your recipient starts to read your message on the computer screen and then is called away, it will be in full view of anyone who walks by.

• Reread your messages for the proper tone before pressing "send." E-mail is usually written in a conversational manner, but it lacks the voice and body language cues that are a big part of personal communication. For this reason, the tone of E-mail messages is subject to misinterpretation.

In general, be careful about what you say. Your messages are not secure. In a growing number of companies, upper management retains the right to read employees' E-mail if it believes there is a good reason to do so. And of course the system administrator has access to everyone's E-mail.

MAKING EFFECTIVE PRESENTATIONS

At some point in your career you'll probably be asked to give a presentation. Many good books have been written about the subject (see the Recommended Reading section in the back of this book), but here's a quick summary just in case your boss asks you to speak at a meeting next week.

Preparing Your Notes

Before you begin to write out the notes for your talk, you need to do a little research and planning.

Clarify Your Message and Your Goal. In preparing an oral presentation, as in writing a memo, letter, or report, you must first have a clear understanding of what you will say and why you are saying it. If you are at all vague or unsure about your assignment, talk it over with your boss until you feel confident that you understand. This step is crucial to a successful presentation.

Know Your Audience. Find out exactly who you'll be speaking to. Learn everything you can about your audience. Why? Because you need to find out what they already know about your topic so you can tailor your message. If you're too technical and use terms and jargon your listeners don't understand, you'll lose them. If you oversimplify and tell them what they already know, they'll fall asleep.

You'll also need to know how your listeners feel about your topic, and what it means to them. Will you be facing a hostile audience or one that is supportive of your message? Will you be persuading people to your point of view, or will you simply be giving them information they need to know? Once you know these things, you can proceed to the key question that you will build your presentation on: What's in it for your listeners? The more you can focus your talk on the special (and selfish) interests of your audience, the more effective it will be.

Find out how long you'll be expected to talk, including any time allowed for a question-and-answer session at the end. Later, when you're rehearsing your talk, you'll want to pay close attention to its length.

Plan Your Approach. A basic principle of good presentations is to capture the attention of your audience at the very beginning of your talk. The standard opening used to be a joke or two, but since jokes can fall flat or offend people, it's better to start with an anecdote—a story illustrating something relevant to your main points. Or you might try to come up with a "grabber," some amazing facts or statistics that drive home the essence of your message.

The classic advice on structuring speeches and presentations is "tell them what you're going to tell them, tell them, and then tell them what you told them." In other words, a little repetition is a good thing, because people remember only about 10 percent of what they hear.

Try to keep your message to three or four main points. If you pack in too much, your audience will get lost. It's a good idea to number these points and then repeat those numbers as you go along. This gives listeners something to cue in to, and—you hope—structure their notes on.

Find words and ways to make these points as clear as possible. Use short, simple words and short sentences. Don't include information that is not necessary to support your main points; you will lose your audience's attention if you do. Whenever you can, use specific words and examples, not generalities. You're trying to paint a picture in their minds, and abstract words and thoughts have a tendency to go right past people. Give the listeners something concrete to hang on to and remember. Real-life examples can be very effective, especially if the audience can relate to them directly.

Tell people what your message is, right at the start. The main part of your talk will focus on the evidence or arguments you'll make to support those points. Also tell them what actions, if any, you will expect from them.

As you go along, insert introductions before your main points to let people know which ideas are coming. Use words like "And now I'll turn to the most important . . . ," "The next crucial fact is . . . ," and similar statements to catch the listeners' attention and help them focus on where you are.

If you have to talk about statistics—sales or production figures, the capabilities of equipment, or anything else that can be put into numbers—figure out ways to make them more interesting or real to people. Translate statistics into numbers that your audience can relate to, such as so many pounds or dollars per person in the United States, or use charts and graphs to show rather than describe large numbers (see Using Visuals in the next section).

Giving the Talk

The first few times you do presentations, you may want to write out your entire talk on paper to give you a solid foundation for what you want to say. But you should never read from those pages during your talk. Instead, jot down your main talking points on index cards—the 5-by-7-inch size is good—and refer to the cards as needed. Don't write down whole sentences, just key words and phrases to jog your memory. Print, using a heavy black pen, and use red to underline your most important points. If you rehearse a few times and really understand what you want to say, the cards will be sufficient to help you along. You'll be more confident, and your talk will be much livelier and more interesting to listen to than if you stand up and read full sentences from a sheaf of rumpled papers.

Don't worry if you have to pause every once in a while to refer to your cards. Pauses are an effective way to hold the attention and interest of your audience—even people who were daydreaming will take an interest if there is a sudden silence. But do try to avoid saying "uumm . . ." too often.

Another good technique for holding your listeners' attention is to use the words *you* and *your* liberally. It gets people involved and reassures them that you have their interests and concerns at heart.

Be sure to make eye contact at some point with every person in the audience. Look for some friendly faces and return to them throughout your talk—seeing them will make you feel less nervous.

Using Visuals. Depending on your talk, you may want to use visual aids, such as flipcharts, overhead slides (also called viewgraphs), 35-mm slides, or computerized "slides." Research has shown that adding visual aids greatly increases interest and helps people remember what was said. If you have a lot of numbers and statistics to present, showing charts and graphs can help your audience "see" your points. Visual messages are easier to absorb and remember than verbal ones.

You can make simple overhead slides using transparency film (make sure it's the right kind) in your printer or photocopy machine—ask how to do this if you don't know. The use of 35-mm slides and slide projectors is being rapidly replaced by personal computers hooked up to a digital display unit that sits on top of an overhead projector. Presentation software is available that lets you create "slides" for direct projection from your computer.

A few basic principles apply to slides and viewgraphs. First, keep the information on each slide to no more than six lines, and use words and phrases, not complete sentences. Think of the slides as talking points, not as the entire presentation. Also make sure the typeface is clear and large enough for people to read. Second, use color whenever you can but keep the overall effect simple. If you get too complex and flashy, you'll divert people's attention from your main message. Third, keep the number of slides to a minimum—the fewer, the better.

When you're finished showing one slide, turn the machine off. Turn it on again when you're ready to start the next one. This is another technique for keeping people's attention.

Many speakers pass out hard copies of their presentation before they start to talk. This is a mistake—people will immediately read it through and be bored before you even start. Always hand out copies at the end of your talk, to give the audience something to refer to later.

Don't forget to allow some time to check out the room and the equipment, including microphones and air-conditioning, at least a half hour before your talk begins. Make sure, also, that you know how to use any machines you'll need—don't assume that one projector is just like another.

The Conclusion. Let people know when you've reached the end by saying something like "In conclusion . . ." or "Finally, . . ." This will almost certainly grab their attention. Then restate your main messages and supporting arguments or evidence one more time. Don't spend a long time on this—a minute or two is sufficient.

The Question-and-Answer Period. Most presentations end with the speaker asking "Any questions?" The best way to prepare for this part of your talk is to anticipate what questions are likely to be asked; you might get your boss or a colleague to help you. Create a list of these questions and think about how you would answer them. This will give you the head start you'll need to feel comfortable later. Keep in mind that you can use these questions to reemphasize the main points of your talk. Truly skilled presenters can take questions and turn them around to meet their own needs. Look for this technique the next time you're watching a politician being interviewed on TV.

Avoiding Nervousness. Only experience will help you avoid the jitters before you get up to talk. When you've done this once or twice, you'll find it's not as scary as you first imagined. One expert advises keeping your hands and arms below your heart level to minimize shaking. But the best way to control your fear is to rehearse your presentation thoroughly and to make sure you're as well prepared as you can possibly be. If you're confident about your subject matter, the rest will come more easily.

Looking Your Best. You'll probably be speaking to people who are older than you are, so it's especially important that you dress conservatively. You will want your listeners to take you seriously and not focus on your age, so don't give them a reason to. Wear subdued colors and dress up just a little bit more than you would for a normal day at work. Keep your hairstyle and (if you're a woman) your makeup conservative and limit any jewelry to one or two simple pieces. Watch your language as well—stick to more formal English to be on the safe side. Again, you don't want to emphasize your youth by using slang or current expressions.

8

What to Expect from Performance Reviews

At some point in your first year on the job, your manager will evaluate your performance. Many companies require a first appraisal after ninety days, presumably to correct deficiencies or misunderstandings before they become big problems.

Increasingly, however, companies are using this early appraisal to identify and dismiss poor performers before investing too much in training and development. In today's cost-conscious companies, every person must contribute in some way to profits, not losses. You need to make sure your boss views you as a benefit, not a drain.

You may also be evaluated after six months, and again after one year on the job. One of these reviews may be a performance review, and the other may be a performance review combined with a salary review. Some companies, though, have just one combined review a year. Here we'll discuss what you should expect at your review and how you can prepare for it. We'll also talk about what you can expect in the way of pay raises and explain how they work.

Sometimes your biggest problem will be to get your boss to give you a review at all—most managers dread the process and will put it off as long as possible. Why? Because—

- They're uncomfortable discussing performance problems, even minor ones.
- They see it as time-consuming, especially if they have many employees.
- They may not like the content and scope of the review form, which was probably put together by the Human Resources Department without their input.
- They're afraid that employees will take even the most minor critical comments personally, resulting in resentment and low morale.
- They haven't received training on how to give effective reviews.
- They've failed to give informal feedback during the preceding weeks and months, so that the review becomes a confrontation, not a discussion.

Even if it hurts a little, you need to get as much as you can from these sessions, especially if your boss seems hesitant. If your review lasts five minutes and consists of your boss saying what a great job you're doing, you'll miss out on getting information that could help you later. No one does a perfect job, especially during the first year. It will be better to hear now about areas that need improvement rather than risk being blindsided by your next boss, who may not be as reluctant to bring up problems.

PREPARING FOR YOUR FIRST REVIEW

Once you've made a few friends in your office, ask them how performance reviews are handled. Find out if the reviews are taken seriously and used to justify promotions and raises, or if they're merely a formality, to be done quickly and filed away, never to be referred to again.

Also find out, if you can, how ratings are given. Most review forms assign ratings such as *superior* (or *outstanding*), *excellent*, *good* (or *satisfactory*), *fair* (or *less than satisfactory*), and *poor*. Others try to be more objective, with wording like *exceeds standards, meets standards, sometimes meets standards,* and *fails to meet standards.* Different managers interpret ratings in different ways. In your office, a *satisfactory* rating may mean you are doing well, or it may be the kiss of death. A manager who doesn't want to hurt anyone's feelings will freely give *outstanding* ratings, whereas a manager who wants to be totally fair and objective may rarely do so. Some companies, in an attempt to ensure fairness, require managers to limit the number of *outstanding* and *poor* ratings to a certain percentage of employees, such as one in ten.

You'll need to make sure that your boss is aware of all of your contributions and accomplishments. The performance review form will probably contain a section for you to note these achievements. When the time comes, you probably won't be able to remember all of them, so you should start now to keep a file or set aside a space in your notebook to record what you've done. Managers have short memories and a lot on their minds; don't assume yours will remember—or even notice—everything you've done. This is not the time to undersell yourself by being too modest or thinking everyone knows your accomplishments. The performance review is a great time to blow your own horn.

Also be sure to keep a running list throughout the year of things you'd like to do that relate to your career goals, such as receiving specialized training, and any projects or assignments you'd like to work on. You'll be prepared when your boss asks you what you'd like to be doing in the coming year, and he or she will be impressed that you already know.

THE APPRAISAL PROCESS

Most performance review forms consist of four parts: (1) your accomplishment of the objectives set forth at your previous review, (2) your overall performance on the job, (3) steps to be taken to ensure improvement and growth, and (4) goals or objectives (agreed to by both manager and employee) for the next appraisal period. Once those goals are set, it's up to you to see that they are completed—don't expect any reminders. At the end of the review period, your manager or the Human Resources Department will probably give you a self-evaluation form to complete.

Ratings and How They Work

The form may ask you to rate yourself on the same factors that your boss will use; be as honest and realistic as you can on these items. It may be tempting to rate yourself *outstanding* on every item, but it's a rare person who truly merits such ratings. On the other hand, don't be overly modest and give yourself low ratings. It's unlikely that your boss will do the same, but you don't want to make it easy for her. If you stop and think about each item, and answer it objectively, your boss will be more comfortable discussing things with you. You'll probably find that the two of you will agree on the areas that need improvement.

You'll probably be given a deadline for completing the form and handing it in to your manager. He or she will then complete the manager's form and set a time to discuss it with you. Usually all reviews must be completed by a certain date, especially if pay increases are tied to the results of the review.

Carey recalls, "My boss at my first job was notorious for not getting performance reviews done on time—he was often six or seven months late! HR's rule was that reviews had to be turned in within three days of the employee's anniversary date. Even if the boss gave you a raise, it wouldn't show up in your paycheck until he decided to do your review and turn it in. This made a lot of people mad, including me. In my third year, he pulled the same thing again. I asked him many times to give me my review, but he never would. I finally had to complain to HR, and he did the review a few days later. If this happens to you, be sure to talk with your boss at least a couple of times about it before going to HR."

You may be evaluated on several different factors and in several different ways. Some forms focus on behavioral traits, such as initiative, dependability, resourcefulness, and so on. Others require a narrative evaluation followed by a single rating, such as *outstanding* or *satisfactory*. Still others are tied to personal and group sales figures or productivity levels. Some forms only rate job performance and achievement of goals or objectives. A few companies determine pay increases by peer rankings—that is, they ask the manager to compare the performance of all employees and to come up with an ordered ranking, such as 1 through 10. If you're at the top, you'll get the highest percentage increase.

All of these rating systems have problems. The first is known as the halo effect, which means that your manager is likely to rate you higher because he or she likes you, regardless of your performance. The reverse, known as the horns effect, also happens—if your manager doesn't seem to like you, you will receive lower ratings even if your performance is on a par with someone who received good ratings.

Another problem is known as the recency effect. Your manager may give you lower ratings than you deserve because of a negative incident that happened close to review time. The good work you did earlier in the year is overshadowed by that recent event.

Still another review error happens when managers tend to rate people higher because they have similar personal interests or backgrounds, or rate them lower if similarities are few. Also, people who are outgoing and involved are often perceived to be better workers than those who are shy and reserved. Sometimes a manager's comfort level with a person, personalitywise, can affect perceptions of competence.

Your manager might rate you higher than you deserve because he or she doesn't want to upset or discourage you. The problem here is that when other employees who have worked hard find out what's going on, they get demoralized and wonder why they put forth the effort if it doesn't make a difference at review time. Another problem may come in the following year. Your work has not improved, and the manager, who gave you a lenient rating before, finally has to come down hard. At that point, you wonder what happened—after all, your performance hasn't changed from last year, so why the bad rating?

Some managers are so stingy and strict with their ratings that it seems they can never be pleased. This approach affects everyone's morale, regardless of performance level. In fact, this type of manager is often tougher on the good workers than on the average ones, thinking that management's high expectations will encourage them to produce even greater results. A few managers will refuse to give the top rating to anyone, believing that only one person in a lifetime could possibly deserve such an honor.

Remember that a manager considers two things when evaluating your performance: the quality of your work and your attitude. As Chapter 2 explained, a positive attitude is a basic part of your job, whether it's mentioned or not. You can do an outstanding job in terms of work quality and productivity, but if you have a negative attitude, your performance review will be less than glowing.

There is one other aspect of ratings that you should be aware of. Some managers will give you an *outstanding* rating on your first review because they felt you had a lot to learn and adjust to and came through quite well. By the second review, however, you may receive the next lower rating for the same category, even though you've now mastered the basic work. Management's reasoning is that the circumstances have changed. After a year or so, your boss determines that you are now performing the job at the average level expected from almost anyone after that amount of time. To get an *outstanding* rating now, you'll have to go above and beyond the basic job description. If your rating is lowered, ask for clarification—just to make sure you haven't really fallen back in terms of performance.

One last word of warning. Some companies have begun asking employees to rate their bosses. You'll never know for sure who will see your rating, so unless you can be absolutely assured of anonymity, keep your responses as tame as possible. Such reviews are appealing to the people in Human Resources and upper management, but their built-in flaw—the unlikelihood that people will risk offending their boss—limits their usefulness.

Types of Appraisals

The most troublesome appraisal method uses behavioral or personality traits to rate performance. Problems arise when your definition of *dependability* or *shows initiative* is different from your boss's, but you're not sure how. If your form contains these kinds of traits, and your boss rates you low on any of them, try to get real-life examples of what he considers to be top performance in those areas. You may have thought you were being careful by asking your boss's permission for every action you took, whereas he figured you were ready to make most decisions alone and therefore rated you low on *shows initiative*. Examples like this one reveal how performance reviews can be helpful in clarifying expectations. Or if your boss doesn't give you much feedback day to day, the review is a good time to force her to open up—in a way, she feels it's expected of her at this time. Here are some other behavioral traits and what they often mean:

- *Flexible:* You have a "can-do" attitude and take change in stride.
- *Decisive:* You make decisions, usually right ones, quickly and logically.
- *Works well with others:* People seem to like you.
- *Uses time wisely:* You don't goof off, and you get a large amount of work done.
- *Communicates well (written and oral):* You keep everyone informed, and your meaning is clear; written documents are of professional quality.
- *Trustworthy:* You are reliable and honest.

- *Creative:* You contribute good ideas and find better ways to do things.
- *Demonstrates leadership skills:* You've made some good calls in tough situations, and people seem to be motivated by your example.
- *Ethical:* You do the right thing, even if it's difficult to do.
- *Job knowledge:* You know what you're doing and do it well.

Other appraisal methods focus more on performance-related items, like the following:

- Technical competence/understands job requirements and performs them well
- Ensures that work is accurate and error-free
- Meets deadlines
- Participates actively in team efforts
- Is a self-starter; works with little direct supervision
- Follows company policies and procedures
- Is customer-oriented
- Sees a job through to completion
- Works well under pressure
- Arrives at work on time
- Sets priorities wisely
- Is aware of the need for confidentiality
- Is ready to handle increased responsibilities

During the Review

If your boss rates you lower than you had expected in any area, ask for specific examples of what you did wrong and how you can improve. You may have to push to get these examples. This is the hard part, because both of you would probably rather gloss over any bad news than focus on it. But if you fail to find out, the problem, which is merely an annoyance to your boss right now, may not get fixed and may grow to become a major issue. This is how "surprises" can take place at later performance reviews.

The worst thing that can happen during your review is for your manager to bring up something negative about your performance that is a total surprise to you—she's never mentioned it before. Your boss, on the other hand, thinks she *has* talked about it with you. If so, it's probably been only in a vague way, perhaps at your last review. Try to stay alert to any comments that might be directed toward the way you do things, and ask plenty of questions. It seems unnecessary, but often it's really up to you—for your own good—to draw out this information from your boss.

Believe it or not, some managers will ask you to do your own review, or at least write up something for them to use to create a document for their signature. Since you don't have a choice, be as positive and glowing as you feel you can. The bad part is that you may not get sufficient feedback from such a boss to help you grow in your career.

SETTING GOALS

You may have a boss who sets all your objectives for you. If that's the case, you should at least feel comfortable that you can achieve them. If not, now's the time to speak up, not six months or a year later. Don't hesitate to negotiate on these. Most managers will go along, especially if they feel your concerns are due to your lack of experience, not your unwillingness to do a little hard work.

Goals and objectives work best and are most fair when the manager and the employee work together to develop them, and when the goals meet these criteria:

• They must be *specific*. For example, it's okay to say that you will aim to increase production of widgets, but it's not okay to say that you will contribute to improving company profits— that's just too general. What if, despite your good efforts, the company's profits go down? You will have failed to meet your goal.

- They must be *measurable*. This ties in to the requirement above; your goal might be to increase widget production by 100 per month.
- They must be *achievable*. If you know that it would be almost impossible to produce an extra 100 widgets a month, don't agree to the goal; instead, ask to put in a number that is more reasonable—say, 50 or 75. Anticipate, though, that your boss will expect you to "stretch" a little to meet a goal—it's how you'll grow.
- They should have a *completion date*. A goal should be completed sometime during the appraisal period, which eliminates goals that are really a basic part of your job.
- The number of goals should not exceed seven or eight.

If your boss comes up with goals for you that don't meet these requirements, try to get the goals reworded so they do. This is to protect you later on. If the objectives are on paper, your boss can't say, "I thought we talked about producing 150 more widgets a month, so you didn't make your goal." It's not that your boss is trying to be unfair; it's just that it's human nature for people to think they said things that they didn't.

SIGNING THE FORM

Most performance-evaluation forms require both the employee and the manager to sign them. There's often a space for the employee to add comments after the appraisal is completed, and this is where you can note any disagreements you have with the appraisal. Doing so will not change your rating, but it may make you feel better to express your view, and someone in Human Resources will probably take note. If your boss has a history of giving unfair evaluations, among other weaknesses, your comments may help strengthen any case HR has against the person. Be careful what you say and how you word it, however; if your comments are critical of your boss, you could be creating a very uncomfortable situation.

PERFORMANCE PROBLEMS

What happens if your boss isn't happy with you and your work? In most cases, the problem is something you can fix, once you understand what it is. Many young people have a tough time on their first real job, not because they're not smart or hardworking but because they don't understand exactly what's expected of them. As soon as they see what they're supposed to do or how they're to act, they become quite successful. If you feel confused about what your boss wants, don't let it get you down. You have a lot of company.

Most managers are aware of this and will try to be fair and sympathetic; remember, they want to see you succeed or they wouldn't have hired you in the first place. They would also like to avoid having to restart the hiring process. If you don't improve after one or two discussions about a problem, however, your boss will begin to have doubts. If things continue to slide, he or she will start to lose hope and begin thinking about replacing you. If you keep your eyes and ears open, you'll probably begin to sense this change in attitude. Your boss may become short with you, or start increasing your workload and adding stricter deadlines. Most managers would never admit this, but it would be easier for them if you got so miserable that you just quit. Managers who really hate confrontations (and hate to admit they made a poor hiring decision) can let this kind of treatment go on for months and even years before they'll finally do something about it. You don't need such misery. But there is one thing you might try before you decide to start looking for another job—get things out in the open.

If your boss *hasn't* talked to you in detail about any problems with your performance, try to encourage him to—if only to help you out of this situation. If you can get him to start talking, try your best to sit and listen. Don't become defensive, or he'll stop. This discussion won't be any fun, but if you can save your job and learn something that will help your career in the long run, it will be worth it. If your boss refuses to talk or doesn't tell you anything of substance, you may be out of luck, and there's not much you can do but decide to look for another job.

HOW RAISES ARE DETERMINED

Where Raises Come From

The way raises are set varies from company to company, with large companies likely to have more complex systems in place. Regardless of size, however, a company must usually show a profit for the year in order to have money for pay increases. The size of the profit, along with the state of the economy in general, will determine the generosity of the raise.

If your company has had a bad year, it may give no raises at all. In the past several years, this has been a frequent occurrence in large and small companies alike, which have also had to impose hiring freezes and even layoffs.

Companies also look at the average pay increases nationwide. When inflation is low, as it has been recently, raises are likely to remain in the 3 to 5 percent range. Companies would rather put any extra profits back into the company, in the form of new equipment and other long-term investments, than into generous pay increases. The reason is that they want to protect themselves if the next year or two are lean years. Once a new pay level is established, the company has to add to it each succeeding year. For example, a person making $25,000 who gets a 10 percent raise (amounting to $2,500) now has a base pay of $27,500. Another 10 percent increase (now worth $2,750) the following year (which you'd come to expect, right?) would push up that pay to $30,250. If you consider similar increases for every employee, especially the higher-paid ones, you can see how payroll costs can skyrocket and become harder to maintain year after year. Companies today are more apt to play it safe and not count on continued good years. They'd rather be conservative now than take a chance they'll have to lay off people down the road.

For these reasons, many companies give onetime bonuses in

good years for outstanding contributions, along with a small, cost-of-living-type raise, rather than large percentage pay increases. In this way, they can reward the top performers while keeping base-pay amounts reasonable. If you're ever given a choice, though, between a onetime bonus and a pay increase, it's usually better to take the pay increase, because it will create a larger base pay for next year's increase. The long-term results will outweigh the seeming benefit of even a generous bonus. Once taxes and other deductions are taken out of your bonus, you may find it doesn't amount to that much. Even if you later decide to move on to another job, you'll have a larger base pay to negotiate from than if you had taken the bonus.

These days, it may not be unusual for you to go a year or two without a raise, so be prepared. Employers are no longer thinking of increases as automatic entitlements—each employee must prove that he or she has earned a raise. That's why it's important for you to keep track of everything you do that brings a cost benefit to the company. If your self-evaluation form doesn't include a space for these accomplishments, prepare a brief memo to your boss before your appraisal is due that lists what you've done.

You may be able to get a boost in pay if you find out that most people performing the same work are being paid more. But you can't expect management to give you a raise just because you know one or two people who seem to be making more than you for doing a similar job. Other factors enter in, such as geographic area, time on the job (to an extent), benefits received, the company's profitability, and the tendency for people to exaggerate their salaries. The best way is to check salary surveys conducted by trade publications and associations in your field. Your HR Department may also subscribe to yearly salary surveys of jobs in your metropolitan area, although getting HR to show you these surveys may be a challenge.

Whatever you do, don't tell your boss you need a raise because you just bought a new car, or need a down payment for a house, or a baby's on the way. Raises are given for business, not personal, reasons. Your boss will want to give you a raise if you do one basic thing: help solve your department's problems.

The "Big Pot of Money" Method

Most companies arrive at an average percentage pay increase by (1) seeing what other companies are doing and (2) figuring out how much of the year's profits can be set aside for raises and bonuses. If management decides to give a 4 percent raise, it multiplies payroll costs by that number and hopes that the result matches the amount of profits available. If profits are lean, that number might become 3 or even 2 percent. Most companies hate to do this, because they're afraid they'll eventually lose valuable employees, especially if raises continue to be low, year after year.

Management also keeps an eye on current pay levels for each occupation in the company. If engineers are routinely getting several thousand dollars more at other local companies, management knows that the firm will start losing people and have a hard time attracting replacements. Many factors are considered in compensation decisions, and exceptions are often made for certain groups of people and for certain individuals.

Once a pot of money has been set aside for raises, managers are told what the average percentage increase is—for example, 5 percent. Managers who have ten people reporting to them, with a total payroll of $350,000, will have $17,500 available to distribute for raises. In formal systems, managers must give numerical values to performance review results and then tie percentage increases to those numbers. In informal systems, the manager gives the highest percentage increase to the highest performer and no increase to the lowest performer. In this way, the top performer can be rewarded with a 7 percent increase, while average workers receive something in the 4 to 5 percent range, and less than average performers get 2 to 3 percent or nothing at all. All that matters is that the pot of money available for raises is not exceeded.

Some managers hate to make these kinds of decisions and simply give the average percentage increase to everyone. They tend to view the increase more as a cost-of-living amount than a reward for good work or a motivational tool. The trouble with this approach is that top performers resent it and may leave.

The "Promised" Raise

One of the most frequent problems new employees face is the "promised" raise. During the interview process or at some point early in the job, your manager tells you that pay "will be looked at" at some point in the future—three months, six months, a year. Sometimes a number or amount is mentioned. But when the time comes, you may not hear anything about it. Before jumping the gun, wait two or three weeks after the date you were expecting something. Some managers like to surprise employees by putting the raise in paychecks without telling them, and since the payroll process has a certain lag time, a raise that is effective on June 15 may not appear until the July 1 check.

But what if your raise doesn't show up? If you didn't get the promise in writing, which admittedly is hard to ask for when you're young and just starting out, the best you can do is ask your boss about it. She may have simply forgotten, or you may have missed certain qualifiers she might have included in her original remarks ("if you do an outstanding job," "if company profits look good," and so on). This can be very uncomfortable for both you and your boss, but you should still bring it up rather than suffer in silence. If you say nothing, you'll get nothing.

If raises are meager or nonexistent, and a promotion seems far away, you may have to get more money the old-fashioned way: Look for a better job. Switching jobs is still the best way for most people to get a good pay raise and increased responsibilities.

9

Where Do I Go from Here?

$\mathbf{V}$ery few first jobs are wonderful and lead directly to your ultimate career goals. By the second or third month on the job, you may have started to realize that the job that seemed so right just weeks ago is starting to rub the wrong way. Even if you've accepted the grunt work, the long hours, the low pay, and the range of personalities and problems that make up your job, you're probably having a hard time seeing where it will all lead. It's easy to picture yourself stuck in your cubicle forever, while you watch your friends take exciting-sounding jobs in interesting companies and faraway places.

You can take comfort in the fact that their jobs are probably much like yours. It won't be until your second job that you'll start to feel you're on your way to a real career. That second job may be in your present company or in a new company, and the type of work you'll be doing may be completely different and more rewarding.

Yours is the first generation to start work knowing that lifetime employment with one company is unlikely. You'll probably work for seven or eight companies before you retire or start your own business, something that would have been unthinkable to your grandparents. (Your parents may have hoped to stay with one company but found they could not.) They counted on long-term employment to provide them with a pension to help fund their retirement years. If they changed companies a lot, they'd have little or nothing in terms of pension benefits by the time they were ready to retire. Today's 401(k) retirement plans let workers build up their own retirement savings that they can take with them from company to company, so that staying long periods is no longer essential to building a fund for retirement.

The massive layoffs, downsizings, reorganizations, and buyouts of the 1990s have changed the way people think about their employers. Job security isn't what it used to be, and loyalty to a company is not the virtue it used to be. As a result, people feel a lot freer to move from job to job than ever before.

DON'T LEAVE TOO SOON

Nevertheless, you don't want to jump ship too soon, for several reasons. First, you should think of an entry-level job as a place and time for you to learn the ins and outs of office life, as earlier chapters have discussed. Every office is different, but most have many things in common, and you'll be better prepared for your next job if you can learn the basics now.

Second, your first job will help you decide whether the type of work and the field you're in are right for you. You may have majored in accounting and now realize you're much more interested in marketing, based on what you've seen of accounting departments so far. Or your journalism degree didn't prepare you for a life of writing technical documentation, and you decide that your next job will be in magazine publishing. Or you may discover you have strengths you never suspected were there, and you'd like to pursue a career that would take advantage of them.

Third, even an unhappy experience will help you grow as a person and as a professional. You will learn many things about yourself and your chosen field in your first job (and all your subsequent jobs). It may not seem like it at the time, but you can learn something of future value in both good and bad situations.

Helen Gurley Brown, longtime editor of *Cosmopolitan* maga-zine, said, in *The Achievement Factors* by B. Eugene Griess-man, that one of the most common mistakes people make in their careers is that they "check out too soon. They don't want to do the grubby stuff. They want to get to the top too quickly. . . ." However, she added, people should stay at each job only as long as they are improving their skills. With each move, she advises, try to keep going "ever so gradually up."

Fourth, you don't want to look like a job-hopper. Even though people change jobs more frequently these days, they don't change every year or two. If you stay only six months at your first job, the companies you'll be applying to for your second job will wonder why you left so soon. They may toss out your résumé immediately, fearing that you lack patience or perseverance or, worse, that you have a performance problem. It's best to stay at least eighteen months to two years, if only for this reason. With the right attitude, you can learn a lot about yourself and about the business world during those months. If the job's not to your liking, use this period to soak up everything you can. There are a few good reasons to leave sooner, of course, such as an abusive boss or other factors that make each day a living hell. But if you do leave, expect that any potential employers will ask why you quit so soon. You'll lose points if your reason isn't a good one (and slamming your previous boss or company at an interview is not considered professional behavior).

Before you decide to leave, ask yourself a few questions about your reasons:

- Did you expect to be doing important work by now?
- Did you think your degree or other training would put you ahead of people already on the job?
- Did you think you'd be able to work independently and receive credit and rewards for work well done?

- Do you feel that after all those years of school, you don't need to learn anything new?
- Do you find it hard to get along with your coworkers or customers?
- Do you feel that you should be making more money by now?
- Is it the job that's making you unhappy, or some other aspect of your life?

As you think about your answers, keep the following points in mind.

There Are Few Overnight Successes

You've no doubt heard stories about famous people who spent years struggling before finally making it, even though their rise seemed to us to happen all of a sudden. Even the most successful entrepreneurs of our time spent years gaining the expertise and support they needed to make it big. It's not simply a matter of "paying your dues." It's that all successful careers are built on a foundation of months and years of learning, through good experiences and bad—with the emphasis on "bad." It may be painful, but failure is a powerful teacher.

Sometimes it's not enough to know the right way to do something. All successful people have had more than their share of failures. Experiencing failure helped them learn not to repeat mistakes later on, when errors might be more costly. You'll also learn the value of persistence, another quality all successful people possess.

There's No Substitute for Experience

You may think that your degree and any related part-time jobs you may have had will put you ahead of your office mate, who has no degree but has worked at your company for ten years. After all, that's why you went to college, right?

Over the long term, your degree will take you further than if you didn't have it. In the short term, however, it helped to get you in the door. People who have been in the company and doing its work for several years are still more valuable to management than you are at the moment. This may be hard to take, but it's true. Most companies know that they will probably lose money on new hires in the first year or two, as they spend time and resources on training and management. To the company, you are an investment in the future, not an irreplaceable resource.

There's No "I" in Teamwork

In college, the only thing that counted was your individual performance. Your grades and any honors or awards that came your way were the result of your own hard work and intelligence. In most companies today, individual performance, although still important, has been overshadowed by the concept of "the team." Management in companies of all kinds, from automobile assembly plants to Wall Street investment firms, have embraced the idea that more and better-quality work is produced by small groups of people who have direct control over their particular product or service. Your membership in teams will give you a chance to develop and demonstrate your leadership abilities— skills that will be key to progressing into management positions.

Whether you work in a formal team setup or in a more traditional departmental setting, you've probably realized by now that you can't work alone. You rely on the work of others to help you get your job done, just as they rely on you. If you can't work well in a group, and your need to shine outweighs your need to pitch in for long periods without credit, you will have a rough time getting ahead. All other factors being equal, a manager will promote someone who is "good with people" and "doesn't need a lot of strokes" over someone who can't get along with others. One survey of managers in 1996 revealed that lack of team-player skills came right after poor performance, on the list of factors that hurt an employee's chance of success.

Lifelong Learning Is Essential

Knowing one or two computer programs isn't enough anymore. Every new job you'll have will probably require learning a few more, in addition to keeping up with new releases of the software you already know. Most companies expect employees to learn these programs on their own time, although some will pay for training. If your company does, take advantage of this resource as often as you can; your next company may not be as generous.

You may also need to fill in holes in your formal education. If you now think you might want to pursue a career in marketing, you might sign up for night classes at your local college or university to learn more about the field. Reading books and periodicals devoted to your field or area of specialization is also helpful, if not essential, to future advancement. Postgraduate course work in your chosen field looks great on a résumé and demonstrates your commitment to your career.

You are living in an era that is changing more quickly than any that have come before. Keeping up with the changes will be a basic part of your work life for the foreseeable future. If you can learn and absorb new information easily and quickly, you'll have the edge.

Money Isn't Everything

Money is probably on your mind constantly. If this is the first time you've been on your own, the need for a good-paying job is becoming quite apparent. Since most first jobs don't pay much, it's tempting to leave if you can get more money right away. You may have no choice if you can't pay the rent on your current salary, but in a few years you may want to think twice about letting money be your prime reason for changing jobs.

If you do a good job and keep your eyes open, you may do just as well over the long term if you stay where you are. Patience is a virtue when it comes to advancement, especially if you are considered a valued employee. Are you in a position that would prepare you to take your boss's job if he or she were to leave in a year or so? Do you have friends or mentors in other departments where you might like to work? Lateral moves, as these transfers within a company are called, may not come with much more pay at first but may give you added experience in different areas and make you more valuable down the road. All of this assumes that you like your company and that opportunities to advance are there.

You should know how to spot a dead-end job. Has there been a lot of turnover in the position? Or, just as bad, are other people in your job there for life? Is the grade or maximum pay level low, as in many entry-level jobs that are basically clerical positions? Does your boss show no interest in helping you move ahead after a couple of years? Remember, if you're doing a good job, it's in your boss's best interest to keep you where you are.

If you decide to look for another job—whether within the company or elsewhere—try to figure out what kind of work you would really like to do. You may think you don't have this luxury, and that money must be the prime concern, but you owe it to yourself to look a little deeper. Over time, you will be more successful in work you enjoy than in work you don't.

You'll also experience less stress and frustration if you spend eight hours a day doing what you're good at, not what you hate. Consider a 1996 study by the Wharton Life Interests Project at the University of Pennsylvania. The survey found that children of parents who had more control over their work and enjoyed what they did, even if they sometimes worked long hours, had fewer behavioral problems than children whose parents came home from work stressed and tense.

HOW TO KNOW WHEN IT'S TIME TO LEAVE

If all is going well for you, and your company is in good financial condition, then *you* can determine when it's time to start looking for another job. If your job is going well but you've decided to look elsewhere, you've probably realized that you don't like the company in general, for a variety of reasons. Or perhaps you don't like the field of work you're in and want to try something else. Those are valid reasons to move. But if the reason is that you don't like your boss or coworkers, ask yourself (1) Could the difficulty be me? and (2) Can I be sure I will be better off somewhere else? You should try to face these possibilities before you risk running into the same problems in your next job.

If, however, your company seems to be having financial trouble, and rumors of layoffs have begun, you may want to start looking for another job—"last hired, first fired" isn't usually the rule these days, but it's still a possibility. If you and your boss haven't been getting along lately, you will also want to get your résumé ready.

The best reason for leaving a job is that you've learned all you can from it and are ready for new challenges. Too many people stay in jobs they've outgrown because they feel safe, and they don't have the self-confidence to try something new. These people will stop getting yearly pay increases once they've reached the top pay level for their job—most companies establish pay ceilings for each job. And these employees may be at risk during layoffs if they're no longer contributing added value to the company. Many longtime, well-paid employees were laid off in the early 1990s as companies looked closely at the bottom line.

If you stay too long, you may also be putting your career in jeopardy. For example, Barbara took an entry-level position right out of college. She liked the company—the benefits were generous, the pay increases were regular, and she was good at what she did. She stayed for twelve years, well past the duration for a typical first job. Over the years, her salary had reached its upper limit. She would now like to try something different, but to do so would mean taking a pay cut, which she feels she can't afford to do. Don't back yourself into a corner just because you feel comfortable; the price you pay will probably be too high.

> Felicia recognized a sure sign that it was time to leave her first job: "I started snacking all the time—the work was so boring that I needed candy bars to help me stay awake through the afternoon."

Recognizing the Warning Signs

How can you tell for sure when it's time to go? Here are some warning signs:

• Your annual raise was less than the company's average amount—say, 1 to 3 percent. (Interim raises during your first year don't count here.)

• Your boss's visits with you tend to be confined strictly to the topic at hand; there's little small talk (unless he or she is friendly with everyone). Or your conversations are all small talk and not much about business. Either way, you've noted a definite change in the atmosphere.

• Your coworkers aren't as friendly or helpful as they once were.

• You dread going to work every morning, and you've felt this way for months; some days you're late or call in sick.

• You're no longer included in meetings you were once invited to, or your comments seem to be ignored in the meetings you do attend.

• Your department has been reorganized and you don't have as much work as you did before.

• If layoffs are about to happen, someone in the know quietly hints that it's time for you to start looking for another job.

• You've been put on a performance improvement plan (PIP) or similar program.

Except for the last two items, don't get too concerned if one or another of these incidents has happened to you. It's easy to build a small slight or rejection into a big crisis. But if you notice that the warning signs continue to happen, you may have reason to be concerned. Also, make sure that the source of any personal unhappiness is truly your job. Stressful financial, family, or relationship problems can easily spill over into your work life, and leaving your job may only compound your difficulties, not fix them.

If you're put on a PIP, it's a safe bet that your job is in jeopardy. Depending on the trouble you're having at work or the type of boss you have, this "plan" will either help fix the problem or serve as the required documentation for your firing. In most cases, it's for the latter reason. Why? Because managers dread dealing with employee problems, and they'll do almost anything to rationalize them, ignore them, or somehow try to correct them. When the problem starts affecting other departments, the pressure on the manager begins. His boss tells him to "do something" about it. The Human Resources Department gets involved, and the decision is made to put the employee on a performance improvement plan, or PIP.

A PIP is truly a plan—it spells out what must be changed and gives a timetable for making those changes. It specifies that certain progress reports, usually weekly, be written up and distributed to the employee, the manager, and HR. In short, it formalizes attempts to improve an employee's performance. For many young people, a PIP often serves as a wake-up call, and in many cases performance improves dramatically. But if performance does not improve, as it often does not, the paperwork trail the PIP provides will help to protect the manager and company in case the employee brings suit against them for an unfair dismissal. Many people see the writing on the wall and quit before the PIP runs its course—which is often what the manager hopes will happen. Unless you are truly committed to improving your performance as your boss requires (and you feel your boss is sincere about hoping to fix the problem), you may want to use this time to start looking for another job. Your days at your first job may be numbered.

If you are fired without warning or without going through a

PIP, you may have legal recourse, depending on which state you work in. Most states have laws that specify "at will" employment. This means that your company can fire you without a reason, at will, and you may have little legal protection unless you can prove you were fired on the basis of sex, race, religion, physical disability, or other discriminatory reasons.

If you are laid off due to a reorganization, merger, or restructuring, you'll be unlucky but your self-confidence should be intact. You'll probably be eligible for unemployment benefits while you look for another job. The benefits won't be a lot but will help. You may also qualify for a severance package, depending on your job and how long you've been there; if it's been less than a year, don't expect much, if anything. Be sure to ask to be paid for any unused vacation time. Also ask about any job placement help that might be available.

In the mid-1990s, a bank had to lay off a large number of employees in order to survive as a smaller, better-organized entity. Management decided to spend six months rating each current employee on the four qualities the top executives considered essential for their new bank to thrive: customer service, diversity, integrity, and teamwork. Those employees who had high marks on all four qualities remained, and the rest were laid off.

While you're looking for a new job, consider doing temporary work. Many temporary agencies have been expanding into professional areas, including computer services, legal, accounting, marketing, publishing, graphics, and other fields. If you're in a large city, check the Yellow Pages under "Employment Services" to get an idea of what's available; some of the nationwide firms have Web sites as well. Temp work is a great way to get an inside look at different companies in your area, and many temp positions lead to full-time jobs.

You may hear about temp-to-perm arrangements, in which a person works at a job for three or four months, and if everyone is happy at the end of that period, the job becomes permanent. The benefit to the employer is that it doesn't have to pay a fee to the agency, because the agency recoups its costs during the temporary period. The downside to you is that you could be let go at any time and you probably won't receive benefits during the temp-to-perm period. The upside is that you have three months to decide if you like your boss and the company.

If you decide to work through an employment agency—the kind that finds you full-time, permanent employment—don't get into any arrangement where you must pay a fee, unless it's for something small like résumé preparation. Reputable employment agencies are paid by employers, who use them to cut their own hiring costs. You can learn a lot about the current job market from a good firm, and it usually doesn't hurt to send your résumé, with a letter stating exactly what you're looking for, to reputable employment agencies in your area.

In short, you have four options to consider when you feel you're ready to move ahead:

- Stay where you are, be patient, and hope to get promoted within your own department.
- Stay in your company, but look for opportunities for cross-training or a job in another department, or even in another city.
- Look outside your company.
- Return to college for an advanced degree or specialized training (which can be done in combination with any of the above).

We'll look at the pros and cons of each approach in the sections below. But before you can make the right decision, you should have a general idea of the direction you'd like your career to go. You may still not know exactly where you'll be ten years from now, but you should start moving in a direction that reflects your interests, talents, and personal needs. Once you can answer the following questions, you'll be ready to match your requirements against the jobs you'll be applying for.

• Do you enjoy being in charge, and do you find satisfaction in working closely with others to make things happen? You may want to look for a job that offers you a chance at supervisory duties.

• Do you enjoy seeing the product of your efforts and really enjoy rolling up your sleeves and working hands-on? You may not be happy in a supervisory role, where you are responsible for seeing that others do the work. You may not know for sure until you have a chance at supervision, but keep in mind that many companies today are recognizing the importance of their technical experts and are compensating them as highly as people managers.

• Would you rather be in a small company, where you feel your contributions can make an impact, or would you be more comfortable in a large corporation, where you may have more directions to grow, better benefits, and perhaps greater job security? (See more about small companies in the next section.)

• Is job location important to you? Does a long commute make you crazy, no matter how great the job is? Have you always longed to live in a different part of the country? You have your chance now, especially if you have nothing to tie you to your current location.

• Is there an area you'd like to work in that would help round out your education, or a skill you'd like to develop that would make you more valuable to future employers? If you can identify these "holes" in your background, look for a job that will help fill them, even if other aspects of the job don't appeal to you. Think about your long-term goals and try to fill in gaps while you're young—this kind of experience will be harder to get as you move up.

• If you're already unhappy in your chosen field and have

the courage to change direction, you may want to consider returning to school to get a degree in a different field. This is a big decision that may involve a considerable investment of time and money.

Staying Where You Are

This option is preferred if you basically like the company and you can see opportunities for growth, even if none seems to be available at the moment. In most companies (but not all), management likes to reward and promote people who are committed to the company's growth and success. So if you are doing a good job and feel appreciated, your patience will probably pay off. Don't be silent about your desire to move up, though. You can run the risk of doing your job so well that management will never want to put anyone else in it.

If you stay, you'll also be building toward increased vacation leave and other benefits. People who switch jobs every two or three years usually don't get more than two weeks' vacation because they have to start over again at each company. You may also have to wait a year at most companies to start contributing to (and receiving employer matching funds for) a 401(k) retirement plan, something you should strongly consider participating in. Certain other benefits, such as life insurance and disability insurance, may not cover you until you've been on the job a certain period. Tuition reimbursement plans also usually require a period of employment.

Moving to a New Job in the Same Company

There are two ways to move within a company: One is for a promotion, and the other is for a lateral transfer, which is to a job at about the same level of the one you now have. Lateral moves can be good for your career because they give you experience in different areas of the company, something that is looked at down the road when you're being considered for management positions. Working in several different departments for the first four or five years of your career isn't considered job-hopping; it's considered a wise career step. Another advantage is that you'll get a firsthand look at areas you may later want to devote most of your career to. Even if you later decide to leave the company, your exposure to different corporate functions will make you more attractive to prospective employers.

Let your boss and the people in Human Resources know of your interest in being moved around the company. Apply for jobs that fit your plan, and be sure to let your boss know that you're doing so (she'll probably find out anyway from HR, so it's best to be up front about it). Most companies have a policy of posting all internal openings before they advertise for the position outside the company.

If your company has branches throughout the country (or even throughout the world), you may want to consider positions in locations that appeal to you. Be sure that the job you take will contribute to your career growth, not confine you to some corporate outpost forever.

It will be easier for you to move now, especially if you're single, than later, when spouse and family considerations are more apt to keep you in one place. Do your homework, however; try to find out as much about the local office and the city before you commit to a permanent move. Consider the disadvantages, including distance from friends and family, a possible increase in the cost of living, and lack of certain features that you now count on, such as cultural events, recreational activities, and a favorable climate. Also check to see how much the company will contribute to moving you to the new location; many companies have cut back in this area, so don't assume anything.

If you are able to get a promotion, that will also look good to future employers. They like to see that another company thought enough of your abilities to move you ahead. As with a lateral move, expect that you'll be in your first position for one to two years before anything happens. Management will expect you to prove yourself in the job you have before it will take a chance on giving you a second job. Whatever you do, don't act as if a promotion or a lateral move is owed to you. This is a common error, and managers who have had to work their own way up resent this attitude.

> "Ditch the ladder, catch the web," said U.S. Secretary of Labor Robert Reich in 1996. This advice was one of his five basic rules for new graduates. "Think of a career less as a ladder and more like a web—webs have a center but no top, and a lot of paths connect. Forget the climb—smart workers move along webs, earning more from skills they've gained, not seniority." His other four rules were to stay computer literate; keep learning to retain a competitive edge; network with people in your industry and profession; and learn to work as part of a team.

Moving to a New Company

Moving to a new company lets you have a fresh start in a job that presumably matches your skills and interests a little better than your first job did. Scott Adams, creator of the Dilbert cartoon series, once noted that the cream will always rise to the top, but not necessarily at a particular company. "The cream has to be willing to leave the jar," he advised. Different companies value different traits and skills, and you may have to look around before you find a place where you'll be appreciated. Moving may also be the only way to get a good pay increase, as mentioned in the previous chapter.

You'll probably find your next job the same way you found your first one: responding to classified ads, talking with friends, pinpointing companies you'd like to work for and sending your résumé. One great way of finding the jobs that never seem to be advertised is through networking. Networking simply means getting to know people in your line of work who can alert you to job opportunities at different companies and can provide a wealth of background information as well.

The best way to meet these people early in your career is to join the local chapter of a professional association or organization in your field. Many associations offer job banks to their members and list job openings, in their newsletter or over a special phone line. Attending monthly meetings gives you a chance to hear speakers from many different companies, as well as to meet people who share your interests. Many long-term friendships and career connections begin at these local chapter meetings. If you volunteer to help out on various committees, you'll increase your chances of meeting people who can help you find your next job. Even if your company won't pay your membership dues, you should consider joining on your own if you can afford to. Participation in these groups is one of the best career moves you can make.

You'll need to completely revise your résumé. Devote most of it to your tasks and accomplishments at your current job, because this is what employers will be most interested in. You can safely delete information about college activities and course work unless they have direct relevance to the kind of job you're looking for. It's also safe to eliminate any mention of after-school and summer jobs, unless, of course, they relate to your chosen career. Be sure to drop any information about your personal life and things like interests and hobbies. Most employers don't really care, and your résumé will be more professional if you stick to business. There are many books on preparing résumés and surviving interviews; you probably read a few when you looked for your first job. You may want to refer to these to help refresh your memory on the ins and outs of job hunting.

Always try to find your next job while you're still in your present one; you'll look like a stronger candidate to prospective employers. But you must be discreet about your job search. Try to set up interviews before or after your normal working hours, or during lunch. Most prospective employers will understand,

and will appreciate the fact that you respect the needs of your present employer. Also realize that if you normally wear fairly casual clothes to work and then start showing up in a suit or dress now and then, your boss will probably figure out what's going on. It's always possible that your current employer will dismiss you if it feels you no longer have a commitment to your job.

You shouldn't overlook small companies during your search. Most of today's new jobs are being created in companies with fewer than two hundred employees. Of course, if the company is still quite young—say, only a year or two old—you'll be taking a risk. But if the company grows, you'll have an exciting and potentially rewarding career. The best way to assess a small company is to take a critical look at its founder: Is he or she in it for the power and the glory, or is there a real desire to create something of lasting value? You should also find out as much as you can about the person's beliefs, attitudes, and personality, because you'll be living with them every day.

If you're coming from a large company, you may have to get used to a much faster pace and the need to be much more flexible. It's said that in a small company, every employee is a salesperson, and your interactions with customers will be especially important. You'll also find that you'll be doing several jobs, often at once, with long hours. There'll be an increased emphasis on controlling costs, so don't expect benefits like tuition reimbursement or 401(k) matching, at least while the company is young. In fact, part of your pay and bonuses might be in the form of stock options. Many young people became millionaires at high-tech companies like Microsoft, Netscape, and UUNET because they got in at the beginning and were willing to work hard toward an uncertain future.

Before you get too serious about taking a job with a competitor of your current employer, reread your employment contract. Many have clauses that prohibit you from working for direct competitors or for clients or business acquaintances for up to six months or a year after you leave the company. These clauses are tough to enforce legally, but your company can make things uncomfortable for you regardless.

When you have a job offer *in writing* from your new employer, you can then give your current employer two weeks' notice. But don't be surprised if your boss asks you to leave that day. Many companies are concerned about competitive or proprietary information in the hands of people who no longer seem to have any loyalty to the company. They will instantly restrict access to the computer system and other types of files. They may also feel that the person will be unproductive during those final two weeks anyway. Don't take this personally—it's often company policy.

If you are asked to stay for two weeks, continue to do your best work. The way you act in those final days will be the impression you'll leave behind. In today's business world, you'll never know when paths will cross again. It may be tempting to gloat about your new and better job or tell people off, but be careful not to burn any bridges. Finally, if your boss seems suddenly cool toward you, and you can't understand why she isn't happy about the progress of your career, consider that she may feel rejected, or perhaps even jealous. Think about how you would feel in her place.

Going Back to School

A year or two on the job may have helped you focus on exactly where you'd like to go in your career. Leaving a paying job to return to school is an expensive undertaking, but many people feel the sacrifice was worth it because it made their long-term goals possible.

It's easier if you can complete your schooling by going back full-time, but you'll probably need to take out loans and find someone to help support you, most likely a willing spouse or parents. You might look into night and weekend programs at local colleges or universities. These programs are becoming increasingly available as adults look for options for continuing their education. Most programs are designed for people who work full-time. Also becoming more common are "distance learning" programs, which are usually less expensive than on-site programs. Many graduate-level programs are now available on-line; check the Internet for current sites. Your company's training group (usually part of Human Resources) or your local public library may have directories and catalogs available that describe these programs. One word of warning: Check the accreditation of the programs, as well as the reputation of the accrediting organization, before you sign up. In recent years some accrediting groups have proved to be phony.

See if your company will reimburse you for any of your fees or tuition costs. You may have to be on the job for a certain period to be eligible, and you may be reimbursed on a sliding scale based on your final course grade. A grade of C or below won't qualify you for reimbursement.

SOME FINAL ADVICE

You've probably heard the expression "You make your own luck," but in fact some people do get lucky breaks. They're in the right place at the right time, or they know someone who can get them the job of their dreams. But most of the time the saying is true, except that it probably should be changed to read, "It's up to you to make the most of opportunities that occur."

Although you should stay open to everything that comes along, sometimes a lucky break or an exciting opportunity shows up at a time that isn't quite right. Events in your personal life may be taking precedence, or you may not feel quite ready for the challenge being offered. It's tempting to think that such an opportunity may never come again, but in fact others will. Just don't pass them all up.

You're in Control

If your biggest concern is that you can't handle the challenges a new opportunity presents, keep this in mind: Most of us never approach the upper limits of our abilities; we tend to think we can't do something, so we never try. Don't let your preconceived notions about yourself (perhaps dating back to bad experiences in school) affect how you think about your abilities. Chances are, you will probably do fine. And the nice thing about trying something difficult and then achieving it is that you'll feel more confident about the *next* big challenge.

The single most important thought you can carry with you is that you are in control of your own destiny—no one else is responsible. If you wait for good things to happen to you, you'll probably be disappointed. Be willing to take a few risks—like accepting an assignment that's a little over your head (you think). Anthea Disney, who now heads HarperCollins Publishers, was interviewed by the *Wall Street Journal* shortly after she took the job. She mentioned that she was somewhat apprehensive about her new job, since she had never worked in book publishing. But she said she was ready to learn and meet the challenges ahead of her, comforted by her personal rule for getting ahead: "If there isn't the possibility of falling on your face, you're probably not scared enough to do a good job."

Be open to assignments and opportunities that will teach you new things or introduce you to new people. Successful careers are made up of many small, seemingly insignificant steps, with one event leading to another like a puzzle. People you meet today may have a major influence on your career a few years from now. One young woman interviewed for a job that she was not quite qualified for, but she made such a strong impression with the interview committee that the employer called her two years later, after she had gained some basic experience elsewhere, and offered her the job she wanted in the first place.

It also helps to work with and for good people. As you interview for your next job, try to find out about the reputation of the manager and the other staff members. Your own gut instinct will probably tell you a few things as well, although people are usually on their best behavior during interviews. If you can find a boss who is willing to be a strong supporter of your skills, you'll be more likely to get choice assignments, ones that will give you visibility in the company and a chance to show your strengths. One successful executive who started as a mailroom clerk in his company had this advice: "Work hard to be the most knowledgeable person at what you do, and be a positive person that senior managers are comfortable being around." He adds that there are no guarantees, but reminds us, "Not knowing your stuff and being a pain in the neck is an absolute prescription for failure." Once you have the trust and respect of your management, you will be given assignments that will move you up the ladder. All of this doesn't come from luck but from hard work and people skills.

The Qualities of Successful People

What makes a person a success? Studies of successful people in all lines of work have shown that they have certain traits in common:

- They discover what they love to do and continually work to develop their skills and improve their knowledge in their chosen field.
- They know how to manage their time.
- They know how to concentrate and set priorities.
- They are persistent.
- They are flexible.
- They are patient.
- They have an open mind and are always learning something new.
- They enjoy meeting and working with new people.
- They take risks and aren't afraid to try new things.
- They see and act on opportunities.
- They truly enjoy their work and take pride in it.

You may have noticed that "They make gobs of money" is missing from the list. The reality is that although success usually brings rewards, great wealth is not always among them. Much depends on the field you're in—you've no doubt heard stories about great artists and writers who achieved success, defined in monetary terms, late in life or not at all. In the business world, however, success is usually rewarded financially, with the greatest rewards going to those who have all the traits in the above list, especially in the area of risk taking.

As you move through your career, you'll begin to define success in your own terms. You may use money as a measure of your progress, but you'll be happier in the long run if you understand that power and status aren't everything. You'll be a success in your own eyes if you work to the best of your ability, if you treat people well along the way, and if you get a feeling of satisfaction from the work you do. Go for it!

Recommended Reading

Career Advice

Body Language in the Work Place, by Julius Fast. Viking Penguin, 1994.

Do What You Love, The Money Will Follow: Discovering Your Right Livelihood, by Marsha Sinetar. Paulist Press, 1987.

Emotional Intelligence: Why It Can Matter More Than IQ, by Daniel Goleman. Bantam Books, 1995.

How to Keep People from Pushing Your Buttons, by Albert Ellis and Arthur Lange. Carol Publishing Group, 1994.

Lions Don't Need to Roar: Using the Leadership Power of Professional Presence to Stand Out, by D. A. Benton. Warner Books, 1992.

The 100 Best Jobs for the 1990s and Beyond, by Carol Kleiman. Dearborn Financial Publishing, 1992.

The Right Job: How to Get the Job That's Right for You, by Robert O. Snelling, Sr. Penguin Books, 1993.

The Seven Habits of Highly Effective People, by Stephen R. Covey. Simon & Schuster / Fireside Books, 1989.

Soar with Your Strengths, by Donald O. Clifton and Paula Nelson. Dell, 1992.

Straight A's Never Made Anybody Rich: Lessons in Personal Achievement, by Wess Roberts. HarperPerennial, 1991.

Talking from 9 to 5: How Women's and Men's Conversational Styles Affect Who Gets Heard, Who Gets Credit, and What Gets Done at Work, by Deborah Tannen. William Morrow, 1994.

Taming the Office Tiger: The Complete Guide to Getting Organized at Work, by Barbara Hemphill. Kiplinger Books, 1996.

What They Don't Teach You at Harvard Business School: Notes from a Street-Smart Executive, by Mark H. McCormack. Bantam Books, 1984.

What They Still Don't Teach You at Harvard Business School, by Mark H. McCormack. Bantam Books, 1990.

You're Smarter Than You Think: How to Develop Your Practical Intelligence for Success in Living, by Seymour Epstein. Simon & Schuster, 1993.

Writing References

The Columbia Guide to Standard American English, by Kenneth G. Wilson. Columbia University Press, 1993.

The Elements of Expression, by Arthur Plotnik. Henry Holt, 1996.

The Elements of Style, by William Strunk Jr. and E. B. White. Macmillan, 1979.

Grammar for Grownups, by Val Dumond. HarperCollins, 1993.

Line by Line: How to Improve Your Own Writing, by Claire Kehrwald Cook, Modern Language Association. Houghton Mifflin, 1985.

The New York Public Library Writer's Guide to Style and Usage, HarperCollins, 1994.

Writing That Means Business, by Ellen Roddick. Macmillan, 1986.

Writing with Precision: How to Write So That You Cannot Possibly Be Misunderstood, by Jefferson Bates. Acropolis Books, 1993.

Speeches and Presentations

Get to the Point: How to Say What You Mean and Get What You Want, by Karen Berg and Andrew Gilman. Bantam Books, 1989.

How to Speak, How to Listen, by Mortimer J. Adler. Macmillan, 1983.

I Can See You Naked: A Fearless Guide to Making Great Presentations, by Ron Huff. Andrews & McMeel, 1992.

Secrets of Successful Speakers: How You Can Motivate, Captivate and Persuade, by Lilly Walters. McGraw-Hill, 1993.

Index

visuals, in presentations, 174–75
voice:
    active, 162–63
    passive, 162
    tone of, 37, 88, 143
voice mail, 11–14, 139
    etiquette for, 12–14
volunteering, 20, 62, 85

Wall Street Journal, 212
weekends, working on, 33
Wharton Life Interests Project, 198
whining, 28, 42, 77
"whistle-blower" lines (hot lines), 120
WordPerfect, 136
word processing, 6–7, 34–35, 136–37

words:
    proper placement of, 164
    redundant, 164
    right, 164–66
    simple, concrete, 163
work:
    hard, 56
    quality, 149–50
    school compared with, 24–25, 41
    smart, 56–57
    temporary, 202–3
writing, 154, 159–71
    bad, 159
    editing of, 161–70
    E-mail and, 170–71
    getting to the point in, 160
    talk compared with, 159–60
    tone of, 170–71
wrongful-dismissal lawsuit, 12